Preliminary Analysis:
The Law and Regulations

IDEA 1997

Let's Make It Work

Public Policy Unit

Published by
The Council for Exceptional Children

Table of Contents

Introduction

On June 4, 1997, President William J. Clinton signed into law the Individuals with Disabilities Education Act Amendments of 1997, often referred to as IDEA 97. IDEA is a powerful educational rights law with a long and successful history. More than 23 years ago, Congress passed Public Law 94-142, a law that gave new promises, and new guarantees, to children with disabilities. IDEA has been a very effective law that has made significant progress in addressing the problems that existed in 1975 when P.L. 94-142, the Education for All Handicapped Children Act, was passed. With the recent reauthorization, the IDEA Amendments of 1997 show that Congress is strongly committed to the right to a free appropriate public education (FAPE) for all children with disabilities. Close to 5.8 million children with disabilities are now receiving special education and related services.

IDEA 97, also known as P.L. 105-17, made significant refinements in many parts of IDEA which will impact the way that parents, teachers, and administrators go about the important work of ensuring quality education and early intervention for children with disabilities. However, the new law continues to affirm the basic principles established in 1975 in P.L. 94-142, such as:

- Guaranteeing the availability of special education programming to children and youth with disabilities who require it;
- Assuring that decisions made about providing special education to children and youth with disabilities are fair and appropriate;
- Establishing clear management and auditing requirements and procedures regarding special education at all levels of government; and
- Financially assisting the efforts of state and local governments through the use of federal funds.

On March 12, 1999, the final regulations to accompany IDEA 97 were published by the U.S. Secretary of Education. As a consequence, this document has been prepared on a fast track to assist teachers, parents, and administrators in understanding what IDEA, *both law and regulations*, now require and how the provisions of both the law and regulations impact on services and programs for children with disabilities. This document builds the regulations into the prior version of this publication which addressed the law only (released in January, 1998), and thus becomes the second edition of **IDEA 1997: Let's Make It Work**. In the interest of meeting the very immediate need-to-know of our readers, this publication is defined as a preliminary analysis, and will be followed by a more refined version of this second edition in the near future. Nonetheless, the core content of what the reader needs to know is contained in this preliminary offering.

Regulations provide further agency interpretation of the law as needed, and regulations themselves have the force of law. This further interpretation of law is accomplished through regulatory definition, clarification, and qualification. This document informs the reader about both statutory and regulatory elements for 15 topical areas through an easy-to-read question and answer format. The content of this publication was developed by a team of policy experts, who were able to come together at CEC headquarters within hours of promulgation of the regulations. CEC acknowledges their efforts with abiding gratitude: Pat Guthrie, Jim Hamilton, Hal McGrady, Ross Taylor, Jo Thomason, and Sharon Walsh. Special appreciation is also extended to many CEC staff for their energy and teamwork in shepherding this product to an early completion.

For access to both the law and the regulations, go to CEC's web site at *http://www.cec.sped.org.*

Section 1 - General Statutory Questions

This "General Questions" section presents statutory information (i.e., that which is contained in the law) about IDEA'97 and information about current and historical laws that have shaped how schools provide for the needs of children with disabilities. Regulatory refinements to IDEA'97 appear in the appropriate sections elsewhere throughout this document. These questions and answers are designed to provide the reader with a broad contextual framework for statutory and regulatory information contained in the rest of the document.

Q. What is Section 504 of the Vocational Rehabilitation Act Amendments of 1973?

A. "Section 504," as it is frequently referred to by educators, is the basic civil rights provision that outlaws discrimination against America's citizens with disabilities. Section 504 was enacted through the legislative vehicle of P.L. 93-112, the Vocational Rehabilitation Act Amendments of 1973, and has been amended several times since then. Although it is brief in actual language, its implications are far-reaching. The statute reads:

> No otherwise qualified handicapped individual in the United States shall, solely by reason of his handicap, be excluded from the participation in, be denied the benefits of, or be subjected to discrimination under any program or activity receiving federal financial assistance. (29 U.S.C. 794)

Q. What were the precursors to P.L. 105-17?

A. Many of the major provisions of P.L. 105-17, such as the guarantee of due process procedures and the assurance of education in the least restrictive environment, that were presaged by earlier federal laws, including P.L. 91-230, the Education of the Handicapped Act (EHA) and P.L. 93-380, the Education Amendments of 1974, came to fruition in the landmark P.L. 94-142, the Education for All Handicapped Children Act, enacted November 29, 1975. There have been a series of amendments to the EHA from 1979 through 1994, one of which created a new Part H in the EHA. Under P.L. 99-457, Part H provided funds for state programs in early intervention services for infants and toddlers with disabilities from birth through 2 years of age. The EHA amendments of 1990, P.L. 101-476, renamed the statute as the Individuals with Disabilities Education Act (IDEA).

Q. What is Public Law 105-17?

A. Public Law (P.L.) 105-17, the Individuals with Disabilities Education Act Amendments of 1997, is legislation passed by the United States Congress and signed into law by President William J. Clinton on June 4, 1997. The "105" indicates that this law was passed by the 105th Congress. The "17" indicates that this law was the 17th to be passed by the 105th Congress and signed by the President.

Q. To whom do P.L. 105-17 and Section 504 apply?

A. Section 504 is far more general than IDEA. Section 504 applies to all Americans with disabilities regardless of age and is not specific to education. P.L. 105-17 applies only to children with disabilities, ages birth through 21, who meet specific eligibility requirements under that law and is limited to educational services, protections and procedures.

Section 504, therefore, overlaps with IDEA in that it also applies to all children with disabilities ages birth through 21 with respect to their public education, both from the standpoint of the guarantee of an appropriate special education, and from the standpoint of sheer regular program accessibility. All children with disabilities who are eligible for services under P.L. 105-17 are also protected under Section 504, but it is important to recognize that children who are not eligible under P.L. 105-17 may indeed be children with disabilities who are eligible for protection under Section 504. Close coordination has therefore been maintained between P.L. 105-17 provisions and regulations and the Section 504 regulations.

Q. What are the purposes of the P.L. 105-17 amendments to IDEA?

A. The amendments to IDEA in P.L. 105-17 can be said to have five purposes:

- Give professionals, especially teachers, more influence and flexibility, and school administrators and policymakers lower costs in the delivery of education to children with disabilities.
- Enhance the input of parents of children with disabilities in the decision making that affects their child's education.
- Make schools safer.
- Place the emphasis on what is best educationally for children with disabilities, rather than on paperwork for paperwork's sake.
- Consolidate and target discretionary programs to strengthen the capacity of America's schools to effectively serve children, including infants and toddlers, with disabilities.

Q. How are children with disabilities defined for purposes of P.L. 105-17?

A. Children with disabilities are defined by the Act as a child:

- With mental retardation, hearing impairments (including deafness), speech or language impairments, visual impairments (including blindness), serious emotional disturbance, orthopedic impairments, autism, traumatic brain injury, other health impairments, or specific learning disabilities; and
- Who, by reason thereof, require special education and related services.

(*Note*: Children ages 3 through 9 may be defined as having developmental delays if their state and LEA allow this designation.)

This definition establishes a two-pronged criterion for determining child eligibility under the Act. The first is whether the child actually has one or more of the disabilities listed. The second is whether the child requires special education and related services. Not all children who have a disability require special education; many are able to and should attend school without any program modification.

Q. What is the current federal definition of specific learning disability under P.L. 105-17?

A. The Act defines "specific learning disability" as:

> a disorder in one or more of the basic psychological processes involved in understanding or in using language, spoken or written, which disorder may manifest itself in imperfect ability to listen, think, speak, read, write, spell, or do mathematical calculations. This term includes such conditions as perceptual disabilities, brain injury, minimal brain dysfunction, dyslexia, and developmental aphasia. This term does not include a learning problem that is primarily the result of visual, hearing, or motor disabilities, of mental retardation, of emotional disturbance, or of environmental, cultural, or economic disadvantage.

It is most important to take note of the prohibition against environmental, cultural, or economic disadvantage because of the wide-ranging implications with respect to the larger population of children who do not have disabilities, but may experience learning difficulties in school.

Q. If a child has one or more of the disabilities listed in the preceding definition and also requires special education and related services, how does P.L. 105-17 define such special education?

A. Special education is defined in P.L. 105-17 as:

> specially designed instruction, at no cost to parents, to meet the unique needs of a child with a disability, including classroom instruction, home instruction, instruction in hospitals and institutions and in other settings, and instruction in physical education.

The key phrase in the above definition is "specially designed instruction ... to meet the unique needs of a child with a disability." Reemphasized, special education, according to statutory definition, is defined as being "special" and involving instruction that is designed and directed to meet the unique needs of a child with a disability. For many children, therefore, special education will not be the totality of their education. Furthermore, this definition clearly implies that special education proceeds from the basic goals and expected outcomes of general education. Thus, for example, intervention with a child does not occur because he or she has mental retardation, but because the child has a unique educational need that requires specially designed instruction.

Q. How are related services defined in P.L. 105-17?

A. Of equal importance is to understand the concept of related services, which is defined in the Act as:

> transportation, and such developmental, corrective, and other supportive services (including speech-language pathology and audiology services; psychological services; physical and occupational therapy; recreation, including therapeutic recreation; social work services; counseling services, including rehabilitation counseling; orientation and mobility services; and medical services, except that such medical services shall be for diagnostic and evaluation purposes only) as may be required to assist a child with a disability to benefit from special education, and includes the early identification and assessment of disabling conditions in children.

The key phrase here is "as may be required to assist a child with a disability to benefit from special education." This leads to a clear progression: A child has a disability because he or she requires special education and related services; special education is the specially designed instruction required to meet the child's unique needs; and related services are those additional services needed for the child to benefit from special education instruction.

Section 2 - Parental Involvement

The IDEA Amendments of 1997 significantly enhanced the role of parents in the special education process. More than 20 years of research and experience demonstrated that the education of children with disabilities is made more effective by strengthening the role of parents, and ensuring that families of such children have meaningful opportunities to participate in the education of their children at school and at home. This expansion of parental involvement is evident throughout the Act and regulations. For a full discussion of parental involvement in specific areas of IDEA, please refer to sections within this document, such as *Evaluation/Reevaluation, Private School Placements, Individualized Education Programs (IEPs), Mediation, Procedural Safeguards,* and *Behavior and Discipline.* The following section highlights examples of additional requirements related to parental involvement in the development and implementation of special education policy and procedures, parent counseling and training, and use of public and private insurance.

Q. How does IDEA ensure parental input in the development of state and local special education policy and procedures?

A. Prior to the adoption of any policies and procedures related to IDEA, each state must ensure there are public hearings and an opportunity for comment by the general public, including individuals with disabilities and parents of children with disabilities. A majority of the members of each state special education advisory panel must be individuals with disabilities or parents of children with disabilities.

Each LEA must make available to parents of children with disabilities and the general public all documents related to the LEA's eligibility for funding under IDEA. Parents of children with disabilities must be included on the school-based standing panel for any school that has been permitted to implement a school-based improvement plan. The LEA must ensure that parents of children with disabilities are involved in the design, evaluation, and, where appropriate, the implementation of school-based improvement plans. One of the required criteria used by an LEA to approve a specific school's improvement plan must be that a majority of the parents on the standing panel agree in writing to the plan.

Q. What are the requirements related to parent counseling and training?

A. Two examples of where parent counseling and training are addressed in the final Part B regulations can be found under "related services" and the state's "comprehensive system of personnel development" (CSPD). The requirements are as follows:

As a related service,

Parent counseling and training means:
  (i) Assisting parents in understanding the special needs of their child;
  (ii) Providing parents with information about child development; and
  (iii) Helping parents to acquire the necessary skills that will allow them to support the implementation of their child's IEP or IFSP.

A component of the state's CSPD must include a description of how the state will:

Provide for the joint training of parents and special education, related services, and general education personnel.

Q. What are the requirements related to conducting "additional" IEP meetings?

A. Appendix A to the final Part B regulations provides the following guidance on this issue:

Source: *IDEA 1997: Let's Make It Work,* 1999, Reston, VA: The Council For Exceptional Children

In general, if either a parent or a public agency believes that a required component of the student's IEP should be changed, the public agency must conduct an IEP meeting if it believes that a change in the IEP may be necessary to ensure the provision of FAPE.

If a parent requests an IEP meeting because the parent believes that a change is needed in the provision of FAPE to the child or the educational placement of the child, and the agency refuses to convene an IEP meeting to determine whether such a change is needed, the agency must provide written notice to the parents of the refusal, including an explanation of why the agency has determined that conducting the meeting is not necessary to ensure the provision of FAPE to the student.

The parents or agency may initiate a due process hearing at any time regarding any proposal or refusal regarding the identification, evaluation, or educational placement of the child, or the provision of FAPE to the child, and the public agency must inform parents about the availability of mediation.

Q. What are the requirements related to the use of "public" insurance?

A. The final Part B regulations contain the following policy clarification on this issue:

(f)   **Children with disabilities who are covered by public insurance.** *(1) A public agency may use the Medicaid or other public insurance benefits programs in which a child participates to provide or pay for services required under this part, as permitted under the public insurance program, except as provided in paragraph (e) (2) of this section.*

(2)   *With regard to services required to provide FAPE to an eligible child under this part, the public agency-*

(i)   *May not require parents to sign up for or enroll in public insurance programs in order for their child to receive FAPE under Part B of the Act;*

(ii)   *May not require parents to incur an out-of-pocket expense, such as the payment of a deductible or co-pay amount incurred in filing a claim for services provided pursuant to this part, but pursuant to paragraph (g) (2) of this section, may pay the cost that the parent otherwise would be required to pay; and*

(iii)   *May not use a child's benefits under a public insurance program if that use would-*

(A)   *Decrease available lifetime coverage or any other insured benefit;*

(B)   *Result in the family paying for services that would otherwise be covered by the public insurance program and that are required for the child outside of the time the child is in school;*

(C)   *Increase premiums or lead to the discontinuation of insurance; or*

(D)   *Risk loss of eligibility for home and community-based waivers, based on aggregate health-related expenditures.*

Q. What are the requirements related to the use of "private" insurance?

A. The final Part B regulations contain the following policy clarification on this issue:

(f)   **Children with disabilities who are covered by private insurance.** *(1) With regard to services required to provide FAPE to an eligible child under this part, a public agency may access a parent's private insurance proceeds only if the parent provides informed consent consistent with §300.500(b)(1) [Definition of consent under Part B].*

(2)   *Each time the public agency proposes to access the parent's private insurance proceeds, it must-*

(i)   *Obtain parent consent in accordance with paragraph (f) (1) of this section; and*

(ii)   *Inform the parents that their refusal to permit the public agency to access their private insurance does not relieve the public agency of its responsibility to ensure that all required services are provided at no cost to the parents.*

(g)   **Use of Part B funds.** *(1) If a public agency is unable to obtain parental consent to use the parent's private insurance, or public insurance when the parent would incur a cost for a specified service required under this part, to ensure FAPE the public agency may use its Part B funds to pay for the service.*

(2)   *To avoid financial cost to parents who otherwise would consent to use private insurance, or public insurance if the parent would incur a cost, the public agency may use its Part B funds to pay the cost*

the parents otherwise would have to pay to use the parent's insurance (e.g., the deductible or co-pay amounts).

Q. What procedural safeguards are available for children with disabilities and their parents under IDEA?

A. For a discussion of the procedural safeguards that are available, please refer to *Section 8: Procedural Safeguards* of this document. The following is a condensed list of procedural safeguards:

- Opportunity to examine all educational records relating to the child;
- Surrogate parents to represent children with disabilities;
- Written prior notice;
- Notice in native language of the parents, unless clearly not feasible to do so;
- Mediation;
- Due process hearings;
- Procedures requiring the parent to provide notice of the complaint;
- Procedures requiring a state education agency (SEA) to provide a model form to parents for filing a complaint;
- Parental consent;
- Civil actions; and
- Attorneys' fees.

In addition, parents of a child with a disability may:

- Participate in meetings with respect to the identification, evaluation, and educational placement of the child and the provision of a FAPE to the child; and
- Obtain an independent educational evaluation.

Section 3 – Eligibility

IDEA, Part B defines a child with a disability as:

a child with mental retardation, hearing impairments (including deafness), speech or language impairments, visual impairments (including blindness), serious emotional disturbance (hereinafter referred to as "emotional disturbance"), orthopedic impairments, autism, traumatic brain injury, other health impairments, specific learning disabilities, deaf-blindness or multiple disabilities; and who, by reason thereof, needs special education and related services.

A child may not be determined to be eligible under this part if the determinant factor for that eligibility determination is lack of instruction in reading or math, or limited English proficiency.

In addition, at the discretion of the State and the Local Education Agencies, the definition of a child with a disability, for a child ages 3 through 9, may include a child experiencing developmental delays, as defined by the state and as measured by appropriate diagnostic instruments and procedures, in one or more of the following areas: physical development, cognitive development, communication development, social or emotional development, or adaptive development; and who, by reason thereof, needs special education and related services.

Q. How is eligibility determined?

A. Eligibility requires: 1) administration of tests and other evaluation materials, and the determination of whether the child is a child with a disability made by a team of qualified professionals and the parent of the child; 2) that a child is determined to be a child with a disability; and 3) that the disability adversely affects educational performance of the child such that the child requires special education and/or related services. A copy of the evaluation report and the documentation of determination of eligibility must be given to the parent.

Q. What is the developmental delay provision intended to do?

A. It is intended to allow the provision of special education and related services to preschool children and children in the early grades without the necessity of designating a diagnostic category for any particular child.

Q. If the SEA and LEA elect to utilize this developmental delay option, may the availability of the other categories be retained for children ages 3 through 9?

A. Yes. Depending on an individual child's disability and resulting needs, the use of a particular category for some young children may be appropriate.

Q. Are there conditions for using the developmental delay option?

A. Yes. A state that adopts the term "developmental delay" may not require an LEA to use it. If an LEA elects to use the term, the LEA must conform to the state's definition and age range (ages 3 through 9, or a subset of that range); and if a state does not adopt the term, an LEA may not independently use it as the basis for establishing a child's eligibility.

Q. Have there been changes in the regulatory definitions for disabilities?

A. Yes. The terms "deaf-blindness" and "multiple disabilities" have been added to the definition section. In addition, there has been a regulatory change in the definition of Other Health Impairment. This revision now includes the terms ADD and ADHD and the phrase, "a heightened alertness to environmental stimuli, that results in limited alertness with respect to the education environment." Expansion has been added to the definition of autism to clarify that autism may be manifested after age 3.

Q. How is eligibility affected by graduation?

A. The final regulations retain the policy position that a student's right to FAPE is terminated upon graduation with a regular high school diploma, but is not terminated by any other kind of graduation certificate or diploma. The regulations also specify that written prior notice to parents is required because graduation from high school with a regular diploma constitutes a change in placement.

Comments from the Senate Committee

The use of a specific disability category to determine a child's eligibility for special education and related services frequently has led to the use of the category to drive the development of the child's IEP and placement to a greater extent than the child's needs. In the early years of a child's development, it is often difficult to determine the precise nature of the child's disability. Use of "developmental delay" as a part of a unified approach will allow the special education and related services to be directly related to the child's needs and prevent locking the child into an eligibility category which may be inappropriate or incorrect, and could actually reduce later referrals of children with disabilities to special education. U.S. Congress, *Individuals with Disabilities Education Act Amendments of 1997*, Senate Report No. 105-17, p. 6.

Section 4 – Cultural Diversity

America's racial profile is rapidly changing. Between 1980 and 1990, the rate of increase in the Caucasian American population was 6%, while the rate of increase for racial and ethnic minorities was much higher; 53% for Hispanics, 13.2% for African Americans, and 107.8% for Asians. The Federal government must be responsive to the growing needs of an increasingly more diverse society. A more equitable allocation of resources among these populations is essential for the Federal government to meet its responsibility to provide an equal educational opportunity for all individuals.

By the year 2000, this nation will have 275,000,000 people, nearly one of every three of whom will be either African American, Hispanic, Asian American, or Native American. Taken together as a group, minority children are comprising an ever larger percentage of public school students. Large-city school populations are overwhelmingly minority, for example, in the Fall of 1993, the figure for Miami was 84%; Chicago 89%; Philadelphia 78%; Baltimore 84%; Houston 88%; and Los Angeles 88%.

Q. What is the definition of "native language"?

A. The term "native language," if used with reference to an individual of limited English proficiency, means the language normally used by that individual, or, in the case of a child, the language normally used by the parent of the child, or the language normally used by the child in the home or learning environment. In addition, for an individual with deafness or blindness, or for an individual with no written language, the mode of communication is that which is normally used by the individual (such as sign language, Braille, or oral communication).

Q. When must notification be provided in the child's or parent's native language?

A. Notification in the child's or parent's native language must be used in the prior notice, procedural safeguards notice, and evaluation sections of IDEA (Sections 614 and 615), unless it is clearly not feasible to do so.

Q. Are there new state reporting requirements that relate to cultural diversity?

A. Yes. Each state that receives assistance shall now include data on race and ethnicity when reporting to the Secretary on the number of children with disabilities that are being served under IDEA.

Q. Is there a prioritized consideration included in IDEA 1997 with respect to limited English proficiency in determining eligibility for special education services?

A. Yes. In making a determination of eligibility, a child shall not be determined to be a child with a disability if the determinant factor is limited English proficiency.

Q. Is there a special consideration in the development of the IEP for a child with limited English proficiency?

A. Yes. The language needs of the child must be considered as those needs relate to the IEP.

Q. Is there attention to the issues of disproportionality in the new law?

A. Yes. Each state that receives assistance shall provide for the collection and examination of data to determine if significant disproportionality based on race is occurring in the state with respect to the identification of children as children with disabilities. This includes the identification of children as children with disabilities in accordance with a particular impairment, as well as these children's placement in particular education settings.

Q. Are the states required to take action when a determination is made that disproportionality is occurring?

A. In the case of a determination of significant disproportionality with respect to the identification of children as children with disabilities, or the placement in particular educational settings of such children, the state shall provide for: 1) the review and, if appropriate, 2) revision of the policies, procedures, and practices used in such identification or placement. This is to ensure that such policies, procedures, and practices comply with the requirements of this Act.

Source: *IDEA 1997: Let's Make It Work,* 1999, Reston, VA: The Council For Exceptional Children

Section 5 – Evaluation and Reevaluation

Before the initial provision of special education and related services, a child must receive a "full and individual initial evaluation." There are two purposes to this evaluation: (a) to determine whether a child is a child with a disability; and (b) to determine the educational needs of the child. A reevaluation must be conducted for a child with a disability if conditions warrant a reevaluation, or if the child's parent or teacher requests a reevaluation, but at least once every 3 years. If the IEP team and other qualified professionals, as appropriate, determine that no additional data are needed to determine whether a child continues to be a child with a disability, the LEA shall not be required to conduct such an assessment unless the child's parent requests it.

Q. What overall considerations must govern the evaluation process?

A. As part of any initial evaluation, if appropriate, the IEP team and other qualified professionals shall:

- Review existing evaluation data on the child, including evaluation and information provided by the parents of the child; current classroom-based assessments and observations; and teacher and related services providers' observations; and
- On the basis of that review, and input from the child's parents, identify what additional data, if any, are needed to determine:
    - whether the child has a particular category of disability;
    - the present levels of performance and educational needs of the child; and
    - whether the child needs special education and related services.

Q. What are the requirements when conducting an evaluation or reevaluation?

A. The requirements include:

- A variety of assessment tools and strategies must be used to gather relevant functional and developmental information about the child, including information provided by the parent.
- No single procedure can be used as the sole criterion in deciding whether or not a child has a disability, or in determining an appropriate educational program for the child.
- Technically sound instruments must be used that may assess the relative contribution of cognitive, behavioral, physical, or developmental factors.
- Tests and other evaluation materials must be:
    - selected and administered so as not to be discriminatory on either a racial or a cultural basis; and
    - provided and administered in the child's native language or other mode of communication, unless it is clearly not feasible to do so.
- Any standardized tests that are given to the child:
    - have been validated for the specific purpose for which they are used;
    - are administered by trained and knowledgeable personnel; and
    - are administered in accordance with any instructions provided by the producer of such tests.
- The child must be assessed in all areas of suspected disability.
- Assessment tools and strategies that provide relevant information that directly assist persons in determining the educational needs of the child must be provided.

Q. How and by whom are final eligibility determinations made?

A. Upon completion of the administration of tests and other evaluation materials, a team of qualified professionals and the parent of the child shall determine: 1) whether or not the child is a child with a disability; and 2) that the disability adversely affects the educational performance of the child such that the child requires special education and related services. A copy of the evaluation report and the documentation of determination of eligibility must be given to the parent.

Source: *IDEA 1997: Let's Make It Work,* 1999, Reston, VA: The Council For Exceptional Children

Q. Is there a prioritized consideration in the determination of eligibility of special education services included in IDEA 1997?

A. Yes. In making a determination of eligibility, a child shall not be determined to be a child with a disability if the determinant factor is lack of instruction in reading, math, or limited English proficiency.

Q. Do parents of a child with a disability have the right under this part to obtain an independent educational evaluation of the child?

A. Yes. A parent who disagrees with an evaluation obtained by the public agency has the right to an independent educational evaluation. See *Section 8: Procedural Safeguards* of this document for a more detailed answer.

Q. Must the evaluation process be followed prior to determining that a child with a disability as defined in IDEA is no longer eligible for special education and related services?

A. Yes. Before it can be determined that a child is no longer eligible under IDEA, an evaluation must be conducted according to these requirements. However, reevaluation is not required before the termination of a student's eligibility under Part B of the Act due to graduation with a regular high school diploma, or exceeding the age eligibility for FAPE under state law.

Q. What overall considerations must govern the reevaluation process?

A. As part of any reevaluation, the IEP team, and other qualified professionals, as appropriate, shall:

- Review existing evaluation data on the child, including evaluation and information provided by the parents of the child, current classroom-based assessments and observations, and teacher and related services providers' observations; and
- On the basis of that review, and input from the child's parents, identify what additional data, if any, are needed to determine:
  - whether the child continues to have a disability;
  - the present levels of performance and educational needs of the child;
  - whether the child continues to need special education and related services; and
  - whether any additions or modifications to the special education and related services are needed to enable the child to meet the measurable annual goals set out in the child's IEP and to participate, as appropriate, in the general curriculum.

Q. What if additional data are not needed to determine continuing eligibility?

A. If the IEP team and other qualified professionals, as appropriate, determine that no additional data are needed to determine whether the child continues to be a child with a disability, the LEA shall:

- Notify the child's parents of:
  - that determination and the reasons for it; and
  - the parents' right to request an assessment to determine whether the child continues to be a child with a disability; and
- Not be required to conduct such an assessment unless the child's parents request it.

Q. Is parental consent required for evaluation and/or reevaluation of a child with a disability?

A. Parental consent is required for an initial evaluation or reevaluation, and for the initial provision of special education and related services. However, a reevaluation can take place without parental consent if the agency can demonstrate that it has made reasonable efforts to obtain consent and the parents did not respond.

Comments from the Senate Committee

The law specifies that parents must provide informed consent before the initial evaluation of a child, but that such consent shall not be construed as consent for placement for the receipt of special education and related services. If a child's parents refuse consent for evaluation, an LEA may continue to pursue an evaluation by using the mediation and due process procedures under section 615, except to the extent inconsistent with state law relating to parental consent. *Senate Report,* p. 18

The committee intends that professionals, who are involved in the evaluation of a child, give serious consideration at the conclusion of the evaluation process to other factors that might be affecting a child's performance. There are substantial numbers of children who are likely to be identified as disabled because they have not previously received proper academic support. Such a child often is identified as learning disabled because the child has not been taught, in an appropriate or effective manner for the child, the core skill of reading. Other cases might include children who have limited English proficiency. Therefore, in making the determination of a child's eligibility, the bill states that a child shall not be determined to be a child with a disability if the determinant factor for such a determination is lack of instruction in reading or math or limited English proficiency. The committee believes this provision will lead to fewer children being improperly included in special education programs where their actual difficulties stem from another cause and that this will lead schools to focus greater attention on these subjects in the early grades. *Senate Report,* p. 19

Reevaluations are to be conducted if conditions warrant a reevaluation or if the child's parents or teacher requests a reevaluation, but at least once every 3 years. Informed parental consent also must be obtained for reevaluations, except that such informed consent need not be obtained if the LEA can demonstrate that it has taken reasonable steps to obtain consent and the child's parents have failed to respond.

One of the most significant changes in the bill relates to how the evaluation process should be viewed. For example, over the years, the required 3-year reevaluation has become a highly paperwork-intensive process, driven as much by concern for compliance with the letter of the law, as by the need for additional evaluation information about a child. The committee believes that a child should not be subjected to unnecessary tests and assessments if the child's disability has not changed over the 3-year time period, and the LEA should not be saddled with associated expenses unnecessarily. If there is no need to collect additional information about a child's continuing eligibility for special education, any necessary evaluation activities should focus on collecting information about how to teach and assist the child in the way he or she is most capable of learning.

Thus, provisions in the bill require that existing evaluation data on a child be reviewed to determine if any other data are needed to make decisions about a child's eligibility and services. If it is determined by the IEP team and other qualified professionals that additional data are not needed, the parents must be so notified of the determination that no additional data are needed, the reasons for it, and of the parents' right to still request an evaluation. Unlike current law, however, no further evaluations will be required at that time unless requested by the parents. *Senate Report,* pp. 18-19

Section 6 - Individualized Education Program (IEP)

The IEP is a written statement for each child with a disability that must be in effect at the beginning of each school year and must be developed by an individualized education program (IEP).

The final regulations in Sections 300.340 to 300.350 discuss the IEP requirements related to responsibility for IEPs; the members of the IEP team; the role of the parent in the IEP process; procedures for the development, review, and revision of IEPs; the content of the IEP; IEP provisions for private school placements and transition services; and accountability. Appendix A, which is cited frequently in this section, provides further guidance, but should be viewed as non-regulatory.

Q. Who must guarantee that the IEP be in effect?

A. In general, the SEA is responsible for ensuring that each public agency develops and implements an IEP for each child with a disability served by that agency or placed in or referred to a private school or facility by that public agency.

However, an exception to this requirement relates to any child with a disability whose parents have enrolled them in a private school, and who will receive special education or related services from an LEA. In this case, the LEA must initiate and conduct meetings to develop, review, and revise a "services plan" for the child. The requirements related to provision of services to children enrolled by their parents in a private school are contained in the final regulations at Section 300.450-300.462 and in *Section 12: Private School Placements* of this document.

In addition, IEP requirements extend to other public agencies (as defined by Section 300.2) that provide special education and related services either directly, by contract, or through other arrangements. However, there are special rules related to IEPs for students with disabilities who are convicted as adults and incarcerated in adult prisons. These rules are located at Section 300.311.

Q. Is there an alternative to the IEP for preschoolers with disabilities?

A. Yes. At state and local discretion, if the parent agrees, a preschool child with a disability may have an individualized family service plan (IFSP). If an IFSP is to be used for a preschooler, a detailed explanation of the differences between an IEP and IFSP must be provided to the parent, and written informed parental consent must be obtained. If an IFSP is used for a preschooler, IEP procedures must be followed and the IFSP must contain the same material as an IEP.

Special Education and Related Services

Q. Are there any major changes in the definition of special education in the new regulations?

A. Yes. According to the new regulations, special education now also includes travel training, if the service meets the definition of special education. Travel training means "providing instruction, as appropriate, to children with significant cognitive disabilities, and any other children with disabilities who require this instruction, to enable them to:

- Develop an awareness of the environment in which they live; and
- Learn the skills necessary to move effectively and safely from place to place within that environment (e.g., in school, in the home, at work, and in the community)."

In addition, the new regulations define specially designed instruction (see question below), and the definition of vocational education has been modified to mean, "organized educational programs that are directly related to the preparation of individuals for paid or unpaid employment or for additional preparation for a career requiring other than a baccalaureate or advanced degree."

Q. What is specially designed instruction?

A. The final regulations state that specially designed instruction means "adapting, as appropriate, to the needs of an eligible child under this part, the content, methodology, or delivery of instructions:

- To address the unique needs of the child that result from the child's disability; and
- To ensure access of the child to the general curriculum, so that he or she can meet the educational standards within the jurisdiction of the public agency that apply to all children."

This term had not been defined in previous federal Part B regulations.

Q. Are there any major changes to the definition of related services?

A. Yes. Orientation and mobility services have been added and defined to mean services:

- *Provided to blind or visually impaired students by qualified personnel to enable those students to attain systematic orientation to and safe movement within their environments in school, home, and community; and*
- *Includes teaching students the following, as appropriate:*
    - *spatial and environmental concepts and use of information received by the senses (such as sound, temperature and vibrations) to establish, maintain, or regain orientation and line of travel (e.g., using sound at a traffic light to cross the street);*
        - *to use the long cane to supplement visual travel skills or as a tool for safely negotiating the environment for students with no available travel vision;*
        - *to understand and use remaining vision and distance low vision aids; and*
        - *other concepts, techniques, and tools.*

Several other changes were made as well:

- A new component has been added to the definition of "parent counseling and training," as follows- "Helping parents to acquire the necessary skills that will allow them to support the implementation of their child's IEP or IFSP";
- A new function has been added to both "psychological services" and "social work services in schools," as follows "Assisting in developing positive behavioral intervention strategies";
- One of the functions in "social work services in schools" has been altered to read "Working in partnership with parents and others on those problems in a child's living situation (home, school, and community) that affect the child's adjustment in school";
- The term "speech pathology services" has been changed to "speech-language pathology services"; and
- "Services provided by a qualified occupational therapist" has been added to the definition of "occupational therapy."

Q. What are "supplementary aids and services"?

A. The term means *aids, services, and other supports that are provided in regular education classes or other education-related settings to enable children with disabilities to be educated with nondisabled children to the maximum extent appropriate in accordance with the LRE requirements under Part B.*

Q. Have there been any changes to the requirements related to assistive technology?

A. Yes. The regulations have added the following new provision: *On a case-by-case basis, the use of school-purchased assistive technology devices in a child's home or in other settings is required if the child's IEP team determines that the child needs access to those devices in order to receive FAPE.*

Content of the IEP

Q. What must be included in an IEP?

A. The following must be included:

- A statement of the child's present levels of educational performance, including:

  - how the child's disability affects the child's involvement and progress in the general curriculum. General curriculum is defined as "the same curriculum as for nondisabled children."

  Appendix A provides additional guidance on determining present levels of educational performance, as follows: *The IEP team's determination of how each child's disability affects the child's involvement and progress in the general curriculum is a primary consideration in the development of the child's IEP. In assessing children with disabilities, school districts may use a variety of assessment techniques to determine the extent to which these children can be involved and progress in the general curriculum, such as criterion-referenced tests, standard achievement tests, diagnostic tests, other tests, or any combination of the above.*

  - for preschool children, as appropriate, how the disability affects the child's participation in appropriate activities.

  Appendix A includes a definition of appropriate activities. It is: *Appropriate activities, in this context, refers to age-relevant developmental abilities or milestones that typically developing children of the same age would be performing or would have achieved.*

- A statement of measurable annual goals, including benchmarks or short-term objectives, related to:

  - meeting the child's needs that result from the child's disability to enable the child to be involved in and progress in the general curriculum; and
  - meeting each of the child's other educational needs that result from the child's disability.

  Appendix A provides guidance on the use of short-term objectives and benchmarks. *IEP teams may continue to develop short-term instructional objectives, that generally break the skills described in the annual goals down into discrete components. The revised statute and regulations also provide that, as an alternative, IEP teams may develop benchmarks, which can be thought of as describing the amount of progress the child is expected to make within specified segments of the year. Generally, benchmarks establish expected performance levels that allow for regular checks of progress that coincide with the reporting periods for informing parents of their child's progress toward achieving the annual goals. An IEP team may use either short-term objectives or benchmarks, or a combination of the two, depending on the nature of the annual goals and the needs of the child.*

- A statement of the special education and related services and supplementary aids and services to be provided to the child, or on behalf of the child, and a statement of the program modifications or supports for school personnel that will be provided for the child:

  - to advance appropriately toward attaining the annual goals;
  - to be involved and progress in the general curriculum and to participate in extracurricular and other nonacademic activities; and
  - to be educated and participate with other children with disabilities and nondisabled children in the activities described in this paragraph.

Source: *IDEA 1997: Let's Make It Work*, 1999, Reston, VA: The Council For Exceptional Children

- An explanation of the extent, if any, to which the child will not participate with nondisabled children in the regular education class and in extracurricular and other nonacademic activities.

Appendix A includes the following language: *While the Act and regulations recognize that IEP teams must make individualized decisions about the special education and related services, and supplementary aids and services, provided to each child with a disability, they are driven by IDEA's strong preference that, to the maximum extent appropriate, children with disabilities be educated in regular classes with their nondisabled peers with appropriate supplementary aids and services.*

- A statement of any individual modifications in the administration of state or district-wide assessments of student achievement that are needed in order for the child to participate in these assessments; and if the IEP team determines that the child will not participate in a particular state or district-wide assessment of student achievement (or part of such an assessment), the IEP must include a statement of:
    - why that assessment is not appropriate for the child; and
    - how the child will be assessed.
- The projected date for the beginning of the services and modifications, and their anticipated frequency, location, and duration.
- A statement of how the child's progress toward the annual goals will be measured; and how the child's parents will be regularly informed (through such means as periodic report cards), at least as often as parents are informed of their nondisabled children's progress. Parents must be informed of their child's progress toward the annual goals and the extent to which that progress is sufficient to enable the child to achieve the goals by the end of the year.

Q. Must a child's IEP address his or her involvement in the general curriculum, regardless of the nature and severity of the child's disability and the setting in which the child is educated?

A. Appendix A provides the following answer to this question: *Yes. The IEP for each child with a disability (including children who are educated in separate classrooms or schools) must address how the child will be involved and progress in the general curriculum. However, Part B regulations recognize that some children have other educational needs resulting from their disability that also must be met, even though those needs are not directly linked to participation in the general curriculum. ... Thus, the IEP team for each child with a disability must make an individualized determination regarding (1) how the child will be involved and progress in the general curriculum and what needs that result from the child's disability must be met to facilitate that participation; (2) whether the child has any other educational needs resulting from his or her disability that also must be met; and (3) what special education and other services and supports must be described in the child's IEP to address both sets of needs.*

Q. Must the measurable annual goals in a child's IEP address all areas of the general curriculum, or only those areas in which the child's involvement and progress are affected by the child's disability?

A. Appendix A provides the following answer to this question: *... a public agency is not required to include in an IEP annual goals that relate to areas of the general curriculum in which the child's disability does not affect the child's ability to be involved in and progress in the general curriculum. If a child with a disability needs only modifications or accommodations in order to progress in an area of the general curriculum, the IEP does not need to include a goal for that area; however, the IEP would need to specify those modifications or accommodations.*

Q. What transition services are required and when must they begin?

A. The IEP must include, for each student beginning at age 14 (or younger, if determined appropriate by the IEP team), a statement of transition service needs of the student that focuses on the student's courses of study (such as participation in advanced-placement courses or a vocational education program).

For each student beginning at age 16 (or younger, if determined appropriate by the IEP team), the IEP must include a statement of needed transition services for the student, including, if appropriate, a statement of the interagency responsibilities of any needed linkages. If an IEP meeting is considering such transition discussions, the public agency must invite a representative of any other agency that is likely to be responsible for providing or paying for transition services. If an agency invited to send a representative to a meeting does not do so, the public agency shall take other steps to obtain participation of the other agency in the planning of any transition services.

Q. Must extended school year services be provided?

A. Each public agency must ensure that extended school year services (ESY) are available as necessary to provide FAPE. These services are defined as "special education and related services that:

- Are provided to a child with a disability:
  - beyond the normal school year of the public agency;
  - in accordance with a child's IEP; and
  - at no cost to the parents of the child; and
- Meet the standards of the SEA."

These services must be provided only if a child's IEP team determines, on an individual basis, that the services are necessary for the provision of FAPE to the child. Public agencies may not limit ESY services on the basis of particular categories of disability, or unilaterally limit the type, amount, or duration of those services.

Q. Is there a protection against unnecessary paperwork?

A. The IEP team is not required to include information under one component of a child's IEP that is already contained under another component of the IEP.

IEP Team

Q. Who are the participants on the IEP team?

A. The participants include:

- The parents of a child with a disability;
- At least one regular education teacher of the child (if the child is, or may be, participating in the regular education environment);

Appendix A offers the following additional guidance on this issue: *...while a regular education teacher must be a member of the IEP team if the child is, or may be, participating in the regular education environment, the teacher need not (depending on the child's needs and the purpose of the specific IEP team meeting) be required to participate in all decisions made as part of the meeting or to be present throughout the entire meeting or attend every meeting.*

For example, the regular education teacher who is a member of the IEP team must participate in discussions and decisions about how to modify the general curriculum in the regular classroom to ensure the child's involvement and progress in the general curriculum and participation in the regular education environment. ...public agencies and parents should discuss and try to reach agreement on whether the child's regular education teacher that is a member of the IEP team should be present at a particular IEP meeting and, if so, for what period of time. The extent to which it would be appropriate for the regular education teacher member of the IEP team to participate in IEP meetings must be decided on a case by case basis....

The IEP team need not include more than one regular education teacher of the child. If the participation of more than one regular education teacher would be beneficial to the child's success in school (e.g., in terms of enhancing the child's participation in the general curriculum), it would be appropriate for them to attend the meeting. ...

The regular education teacher who serves as member of a child's IEP team should be a teacher who is, or may be, responsible for implementing a portion on the IEP, so that the teacher can participate in discussions about how best to teach the child. ...

In the case of a child whose behavior impedes the learning of the child or others, the LEA is encouraged to have a regular education teacher or other person knowledgeable about positive behavioral strategies at the IEP meeting. This is especially important if the regular education teacher is expected to carry out portions of the IEP.

- At least one special education teacher of the child, or where appropriate, at least one special education provider of the child;
- A representative of the public agency who:
  - is qualified to provide, or supervise the provision of, specially designed instruction to meet the unique needs of children with disabilities;
  - is knowledgeable about the general curriculum; and
  - is knowledgeable about the availability of resources of the public agency.

A public agency may designate another public agency member of the IEP team to also serve as the agency representative as long as the criteria included for that team member are met.

- An individual who can interpret the instructional implications of evaluation results, who may be another already required member of the team;
- At the discretion of the parent or the agency, other individuals who have knowledge or special expertise regarding the child, including related services personnel as appropriate. The determination of the knowledge or special expertise of any individual is made by the party (parent or public agency) who invited the individual to be a member of the team; and
- If appropriate, the child. The public agency must invite the student if a purpose of the IEP meeting is consideration of transition services. If the student does not attend the IEP meeting, the public agency must take other steps to ensure that the student's preferences and interests are considered.

Appendix A offers the following additional guidance on other circumstances in which the child may attend the IEP meeting: *"Generally, a child with a disability should attend the IEP meeting if the parent decides that it is appropriate for the child to do so. If possible, the agency and the parents should discuss the appropriateness of the child's participation before a decision is made, in order to help the parents determine whether or not the child's attendance would be (1) helpful in developing the IEP, or (2) directly beneficial to the child or both.*

Further, the regulations state that the IEP must be accessible to each regular education teacher, special education teacher, related service provider, and other service provider who is responsible for its implementation. Each of these individuals is to be informed of his or her specific responsibilities related to implementing the child's IEP, and of the specific accommodations, modifications, and supports that must be provided for the child in accordance with the IEP.

Q. Must related services personnel attend IEP meetings?

A. Appendix A provides the following answer to this question: *Although Part B does not expressly require that the IEP team include related services personnel as part of the IEP team, it is appropriate for those persons to be included if a particular related service is to be discussed as part of the IEP meeting. ... If a child with a disability has an identified need for related services, it would be appropriate for the related services personnel to attend the meeting or otherwise be involved in developing the IEP. ... A public agency must ensure that all individuals who are necessary to develop an IEP that will meet the child's unique needs, and ensure the provision of FAPE to the child, participate in the child's IEP meeting.*

Q. What must public agencies do to meet the requirement regarding the participation of a regular education teacher in the development, review, and revision of IEPs, for preschoolers with disabilities?

A. Appendix A provides the following answer to this question: *If a public agency provides "regular education" preschool services to nondisabled children, then the requirements ... apply as they do in the case of older children* with disabilities. If a public agency makes kindergarten available to nondisabled children, then a regular education kindergarten teacher could appropriately be the regular education teacher who would be a member of the IEP team, and, as appropriate, participate in IEP meetings, for a kindergarten-aged child who is, or may be, participating in the regular education environment. If a public agency does not provide regular preschool education services to nondisabled children, the agency could designate an individual who, under state standards, is qualified to serve nondisabled children of the same age.

Q. What is the role of the regular educator?

A. The regular education teacher of the child, as a member of the IEP team, must, to the extent appropriate, participate in the development, review, and revision of the child's IEP, including assisting in the determination of:

- Appropriate positive behavioral interventions and strategies for the child; and
- Supplementary aids and services, program modifications, or supports for school personnel that will be provided for the child.

Development, Review, and Revision of the IEP

Q. What must be considered in the development of the IEP?

A. In developing each child's IEP, the IEP team must consider:

- The strengths of the child and the concerns of the parents for enhancing the education of their child;
- The results of the initial or most recent evaluation of the child; and
- As appropriate, the results of the child's performance on any general state or district-wide assessment programs.

The IEP team must also consider the following special factors:

- In the case of a child whose behavior impedes his or her learning or that of others, consider- if appropriate- strategies, including positive behavioral interventions, strategies, and supports, to address that behavior;
- In the case of a child with limited English proficiency, consider the child's language needs as those needs relate to the child's IEP;
- In the case of a child who is blind or visually impaired, provide for instruction in Braille and the use of Braille unless the IEP team determines, after an evaluation of the child's reading and writing skills, needs, and appropriate reading and writing media (including an evaluation of the child's future needs for instruction in Braille or the use of Braille), that instruction in Braille or the use of Braille is not appropriate for the child;
- Consider the child's communication needs; in the case of a child who is deaf or hard of hearing, consider the child's language or communication needs, opportunities for direct communications with peers and professional personnel in the child's language and communication mode, academic level, and full range of needs, including opportunities for direct instruction and the child's language and communication mode; and
- Consider whether the child requires assistive technology devices and services.

Q. What is a public agency's responsibility if it is not possible to reach consensus on what services should be included in a child's IEP?

A. Appendix A provides the following answer to this question: *The IEP meeting serves as a communication vehicle between parents and school personnel, and enables them, as equal participants, to make joint, informed decisions. ....Parents are considered equal partners with school personnel in making these decisions, and the IEP team must consider the parent's concerns and the information that they provide regarding their child in developing, reviewing, and revising IEPs. The IEP team should work toward consensus, but the public agency has ultimate responsibility to ensure that the IEP includes the services that the child needs in order to receive FAPE. It is not appropriate to make*

IEP decisions based upon a majority "vote." If the team cannot reach consensus, the public agency must provide the parents with prior written notice of the agency's proposals or refusals, or both, regarding the child's educational program, and the parents have the right to seek resolution of any disagreements by initiating an impartial due process hearing. Every effort should be made to resolve differences between parents and school staff through voluntary mediation or some other informal step, without resorting to a due process hearing.

Q. What happens when a student reaches the age of majority?

A. Provisions for this are described in *Section 8: Procedural Safeguards* of this document.

Q. What is the role of the parent in making placement decisions?

A. Each LEA or SEA must ensure that the parents of each child with a disability are members of any group that makes decisions on the educational placement of their child.

Q. What are the requirements related to reviewing and revising IEPs?

A. Each public agency must ensure that the IEP team reviews the child's IEP periodically, but no less than annually, to determine whether the annual goals are being achieved, and revises the IEP as appropriate to address:

- Any lack of expected progress toward the annual goals and in the general curriculum, if appropriate;
- The results of any reevaluation;
- Information about the child provided to, or by, the parents;
- The child's anticipated needs; or
- Other matters.

Q. What should occur if an agency, other than the LEA, doesn't provide the transition services in the IEP?

A. If a participating agency, other than the public agency, fails to provide the transition services described in the IEP, the public agency shall reconvene the IEP team to identify alternative strategies to meet the transition objectives for the student set out in that program.

Nothing in Part B relieves any participating agency, including a state vocational rehabilitation agency, of the responsibility to provide or pay for any transition services that the agency would otherwise provide to students with disabilities who meet that agency's eligibility criteria. Participating agency means "a state or local agency, other than the public agency responsible for a student's education, that is financially and legally responsible for providing transition services to the student."

Q. When must IEPs be in effect?

A. IEPs must be in effect at the beginning of each school year and before special education and related services are provided. IEPs are to be implemented as soon as possible following the IEP meeting.

Q. Who is responsible for developing the IEP and are there any timelines required?

A. Each public agency is responsible for initiating and conducting meetings for the purpose of developing, reviewing, and revising the IEP or IFSP. Within a reasonable period of time following the agency's receipt of parental consent to an initial evaluation, the child is evaluated and, if eligible under Part B, special education and related services must be made available in accordance with an IEP. A meeting to develop an IEP must be conducted within 30 calendar days of a determination that the child needs special education and related services.

Q. What are the requirements related to parent participation in the IEP process?

A. Each public agency must take steps to ensure that one or both of the parents of a child with a disability are present at each IEP meeting, or are afforded the opportunity to participate, including notifying the parents of the meeting early enough to ensure they have an opportunity to attend, and scheduling the meeting at a mutually agreed upon time and place.

The notice must include the purpose, time, and location of the meeting and who will be in attendance. The notice must also inform the parents about their right to invite other individuals who they believe have knowledge or special expertise about the child. In the case of a student age 14 or younger, if appropriate, the notice must also include an indication that a purpose of the meeting will be the development of the statement of the student's transition services needs as required, and also indicate that the agency will invite the student.

For a student with a disability beginning at age 16 or younger, if appropriate, the notice must indicate that a purpose of the meeting is the consideration of needed transition services for the student as required, and also indicate that the agency will invite the student, and identify any other agency that will be invited to send a representative.

If neither parent can attend, the public agency must use other methods to ensure parent participation, including individual or conference telephone calls. A meeting may be conducted without a parent in attendance, if the public agency is unable to convince the parents that they should attend. In this case, the public agency must have a record of its attempts to arrange a mutually agreed upon time and place, such as detailed records of telephone calls made or attempted and the results of those calls; copies of correspondence sent to the parents, and any responses received; and detailed records of visits made to the parent's home or place of employment and the results of those visits.

The public agency shall take whatever action is necessary to ensure that the parent understands the proceedings at the IEP meeting, including arranging for an interpreter for parents with deafness or whose native language is other than English.

The public agency must give the parent a copy of the child's IEP at no cost to the parent.

Q. What are the specific requirements related to IEPs for children placed in private schools by public agencies?

A. Before a public agency places a child with a disability in, or refers a child to, a private school or facility, the agency must initiate and conduct a meeting to develop an IEP for the child. The agency must ensure that a representative of the private school or facility attends the meeting. If the representative can't attend, the agency must use other methods to ensure participation by the private school or facility, including individual or conference telephone calls.

After a child with a disability enters a private school or facility, any meetings to review and revise the child's IEP may be initiated and conducted by the private school or facility at the discretion of the public agency. If the private school conducts these meetings, the public agency must ensure that the parents and an agency representative are involved in any decision about the child's IEP and agree to any proposed changes in the IEP before those changes are implemented.

Even if a private school or facility implements a child's IEP, responsibility for Part B remains with the public agency and the SEA. See *Section 12: Private School Placements* of this document.

Q. What are the requirements related to the implementation of the IEP and who is accountable?

A. Each public agency must provide special education and related services to a child with a disability in accordance with the child's IEP and make a good faith effort to assist the child to achieve the goals and objectives or benchmarks listed in the IEP. Part B does not require that any agency, teacher, or other person be held accountable if a child does not achieve the growth projected in the annual goals and benchmarks or objectives. However, IDEA does not prohibit a state or public agency from establishing its own accountability systems regarding teacher, school, or agency performance.

Parents have a right to ask for revisions of their child's IEP or to invoke due process procedures if they feel that the good faith efforts required are not being made.

Least Restrictive Environment

Q. What changes have been made to the placement and LRE requirements?

A. The final Part B regulations clarify that the LRE requirements apply to preschoolers with disabilities. Furthermore, the group making the placement decision must now include the parents.

In addition, a new provision has been added to the regulation on placement to indicate that "a child with a disability is not removed from education in age-appropriate regular classrooms solely because of needed modifications in the general curriculum."

Appendix A provides further guidance on the LRE requirements, stating that: *Part B's LRE principle is intended to ensure that a child with a disability is served in a setting where the child can be educated successfully. Even though IDEA does not mandate regular class placement for every disabled student, IDEA assumes that the first placement option considered for each student by the student's placement team, which must include the parent, is the school the child would attend if not disabled, with appropriate supplementary aids and services to facilitate such placement. Thus, before a disabled child can be placed outside of the regular educational environment, the full range of supplementary aids and services that, if provided, would facilitate the student's placement in the regular classroom setting, must be considered.*

Comments from the Senate Committee

Once a child has been identified as being eligible for special education, the connection between special education and related services and the child's opportunity to experience and benefit from the regular education curriculum should be strengthened. The majority of children identified as eligible for special education and related services are capable of participating in the regular education curriculum to varying degrees with some adaptations and modifications. This provision is intended to ensure that children's special education and related services are in addition to and are affected by the regular education curriculum, not separate from it.

Specific day-to-day adjustments in instructional methods and approaches that are made by either a regular or special education teacher to assist a child with a disability to achieve his or her annual goals would not normally require action by the child's IEP team. However, if changes are contemplated in the child's measurable annual goals, benchmarks, or short term objectives, or in any of the services or program modifications, or other components described in the child's IEP, the LEA must ensure that the child's IEP team is reconvened in a timely manner to address those changes.

The new emphasis on participation in the regular education curriculum is not intended to result in major expansions in the size of the IEP of dozens of pages of detailed goals and benchmarks or objectives in every curricular content standard or skill. The new focus is intended to produce attention to the accommodations and adjustments necessary for children with disabilities to access the regular education curriculum and the special services which may be necessary for appropriate participation in particular areas of the curriculum due to the nature of the disability.

The law requires that a child's IEP include a statement of measurable annual goals, including benchmarks or short-term objectives. The committee views this requirement as crucial. It will help parents and educators determine if the goals can reasonably be met during the year, and as important, allow parents to be able to monitor their child's progress. The bill requires that annual goals included in a child's IEP relate to "meeting the child's needs that result from the child's disability to enable the child to be involved in and progress in the regular education curriculum." This language should not be construed to be a basis for excluding a child with a disability who is unable to learn at the same level or rate as children without disabilities in an inclusive classroom or program. It is intended to require that the IEP's annual goals focus on how the child's needs resulting from his or her disability can be addressed so that the child can participate, at the individually appropriate level, in the regular education curriculum offered to all students.

Prior to the enactment of P.L. 94-142 in 1975, the opportunity and inclination to educate children with disabilities was often in separate programs and schools away from children without disabilities. IDEA 1997 contains a presumption that children with disabilities are to be educated in regular education classes.

The Committee knows that excluding children with disabilities from these assessments severely limits and in some cases prevents children with disabilities, through no fault of their own, from continuing on to postsecondary education. The committee reaffirms the existing Federal law requirement that children with disabilities participate in state- and district-wide assessments. This will assist parents in judging if their child is improving with regard to his or her academic achievement, just as the parents of nondisabled children do.

The location where special education and related services will be provided to a child influences decisions about the nature and amount of these services and when they should be provided to a child. For example, the appropriate place for the related service may be the regular education classroom, so that the child does not have to choose between a needed service and the regular educational program.

The purpose of this requirement is to focus attention on how the child's educational program can be planned to help the child make a successful transition to his or her goals for life after secondary school. This provision is designed to augment, and not replace, the separate transition services requirement, under which children with disabilities beginning no later than age 16 receive transition services including instruction, community experiences, the development of employment and other postschool objectives and, when appropriate, independent living skills and functional vocational evaluation. For example, for a child whose transition goal is a job, a transition service could be teaching the child how to get to the job site on public transportation.

The law clarifies that when a child is considered incapable of making educational decisions, the state will develop procedures for appointing the parent or another individual to represent the interests of the child. This transfer of rights is also addressed under Section 615(m) in the law.

The Committee believes that informing parents of children with disabilities as often as other parents will, in fact, reduce the cost of informing parents of children with disabilities and facilitate more useful feedback on their child's performance. One method recommended by the committee would be providing an IEP report card with the regular education report card, if the latter is appropriate and provided for the child.

An IEP report card could also be made more useful by including check boxes or equivalent options that enable the parents and the special educator to review and judge the performance of the child.

An example would be to state a goal or benchmark on the IEP report card and rank it on a multipoint continuum. The goal might be, "Ted will demonstrate effective literal comprehension." The ranking system would then state the following, as indicated by a check box: No progress; some progress; good progress; almost complete; completed. Of course, these concepts would be used by the school and the IEP team when appropriate. This example is not intended to indicate the committee's preference for a single means of compliance with this requirement. Very often, regular education teachers play a central role in the education of children with disabilities. In that regard the law provides that regular education teachers participate on the IEP team, but this provision is to be construed in light of the law's proviso that the regular education teacher, to the extent appropriate, participate in the development of the IEP of the child. The Committee recognizes the reasonable concern that the provision including the regular education teacher might create an obligation that the teacher participate in all aspects of the IEP team's work. The Committee does not intend that to be the case and only intends it to be the extent appropriate. The Committee wishes to emphasize that the "support" for school personnel, which is stated in the child's IEP, is that support that will assist them to help a particular child progress in the regular education curriculum.

Related services personnel should be included on the team when a particular related service will be discussed at the request of a child's parents or the school. Such personnel can include personnel knowledgeable about services that are not strictly special education services, such as specialists in curriculum content areas such as reading. Furthermore, the Committee recognizes that there are situations that merit the presence of a licensed registered school nurse on the IEP team. The Committee also recognizes that schools sometimes are assumed to be responsible for all health-care costs connected to a child's participation in school. The Committee wishes to encourage, to the greatest extent practicable and when appropriate, the participation of a licensed registered school nurse on the IEP team to help define and make decisions about how to safely address a child's educationally related health needs.

The Committee believes that a number of considerations are essential to the process of creating a child's IEP. The purpose of the IEP is to tailor the education to the child; not tailor the child to the education. If the child could fit into the school's regular education program without assistance, special education would not be necessary.

Section 7 - Early Childhood

Section 619 of Part B-The Preschool Grants Program

The Secretary provides grants to assist states to provide special education and related services to children with disabilities ages 3 through 5, inclusive; and at the state's discretion, to 2-year-old children with disabilities who will turn 3 during the school year. A state is eligible for a grant if the state has a Part B grant and makes a FAPE available to all children with disabilities, ages 3 through 5, residing in the state.

Part C-Infants and Toddlers with Disabilities

The Secretary shall make grants to states to assist each state in maintaining and implementing a statewide, comprehensive, coordinated, multidisciplinary, interagency system to provide early intervention services for infants and toddlers with disabilities and their families. A state is eligible for a grant if the state has adopted a policy that appropriate early intervention services are available to all infants and toddlers with disabilities in the state and their families, including Indian infants and toddlers with disabilities and their families residing on a reservation geographically located in the state; and has in effect a statewide system that meets the requirements of Part C.

Q. What requirements are followed when providing special education and related services to preschool children with disabilities under Section 619?

A. The Part B requirements must be followed. All the rights and protections available under Part B are available to eligible preschool children and their parents. Please refer to the rest of this document for current Part B requirements based upon the final regulations that were published March 12, 1999.

Q. What must local school districts do regarding the transition of children leaving the Part C program who are eligible for preschool special education?

A. Local school districts must ensure that children participating in early intervention programs assisted under Part C, experience a smooth and effective transition to those preschool programs in accordance with Part C requirements. By the third birthday of an eligible child, an IEP or, if allowed by SEA and agreed to by the LEA and the parent, an IFSP, has been developed and is being implemented for the child. In addition, the LEA must participate in transition planning conferences arranged by the lead agency under Part C.

Q. What is the eligibility criteria for children under the Part C program?

A. The term "infant or toddler with a disability" means a child under 3 years of age who needs early intervention services because the child:
- Is experiencing developmental delays, as measured by appropriate diagnostic instruments and procedures in one or more of the areas of cognitive development, physical development, communication development, social or emotional development, and adaptive development; or
- Has a diagnosed physical or mental condition which has a high probability of resulting in developmental delay; this may also include, at a state's discretion, at-risk infants and toddlers.

Q. What services does a child eligible under Part C receive?

A. Each infant or toddler with a disability, and the infant's or toddler's family, must have available:

Source: *IDEA 1997: Let's Make It Work,* 1999, Reston, VA: The Council For Exceptional Children

- A multidisciplinary assessment of the unique strengths and needs of the infant or toddler and the identification of services appropriate to meet such needs;
- A family-directed identification of the needs of each child's family to appropriately assist in the development of the child;
- The identification of the supports and services necessary to enhance the family's capacity to meet the developmental needs of the infant or toddler; and
- A written IFSP developed by a multidisciplinary team, including the parents.

The IFSP shall be evaluated once a year and the family must be provided a review of the plan at 6-month intervals (or more often where appropriate based on infant or toddler and family needs). The IFSP must be developed within a reasonable time after the assessment is completed. With the parents' consent, early intervention services may commence prior to the completion of the assessment. The state must ensure that each IFSP is implemented.

Q. What must be included in an IFSP?

A. The IFSP must be in writing and contain:

- A statement of the infant's or toddler's present levels of physical development, cognitive development, communication development, social or emotional development, and adaptive development, based on objective criteria;
- A statement of the family's resources, priorities, and concerns relating to enhancing the development of the family's infant or toddler with a disability;
- A statement of the major outcomes expected to be achieved for the infant or toddler and the family, and the criteria, procedures, and timelines used to determine the degree to which progress toward achieving the outcomes is being made and whether modifications or revisions of the outcomes or services are necessary;
- A statement of specific early intervention services necessary to meet the unique needs of the infant or toddler and the family, including the frequency, intensity, and method of delivering services;
- A statement of the natural environments in which early intervention services shall appropriately be provided, including a justification of the extent, if any, to which the services will not be provided in a natural environment;
- The projected dates for initiation of services and the anticipated duration of the services;
- The identification of the service coordinator from the profession most immediately relevant to the infant's or toddler's or family's needs (or who is otherwise qualified to carry out all applicable responsibilities under Part C) who will be responsible for the implementation of the plan and coordination with other agencies and persons; and
- The steps to be taken to support the transition of the toddler with a disability to preschool or other appropriate services.

Q. Is parental consent required before early intervention can be provided?

A. Yes. The contents of the IFSP must be fully explained to the parents and informed written consent from the parents must be obtained before early intervention services as described in the plan can be provided. If the parents do not provide consent with respect to a particular early intervention service, then the early intervention services to which consent is obtained shall be provided.

Q. What are the transition requirements for early intervention?

A. Each state must ensure a smooth transition for toddlers receiving early intervention services to preschool or other appropriate services, including a description of how:

- The families of such toddlers will be included in the transition plans required; and

Source: *IDEA 1997: Let's Make It Work,* 1999, Reston, VA: The Council For Exceptional Children 29

- The lead agency will notify the LEA for the area in which such a child resides that the child will shortly reach the age of eligibility for preschool services under part B, as determined in accordance with state law;
- In the case of a child who may be eligible for such preschool services, with the approval of the family of the child, a conference will be convened among the lead agency, the family, and the LEA at least 90 days (and at the discretion of all such parties, up to 6 months) before the child is eligible for the preschool services, to discuss any such services that the child may receive; and
- In the case of a child who may not be eligible for such preschool services, with the approval of the family, reasonable efforts will be made to convene a conference among the lead agency, the family, and providers of other appropriate services for children who are not eligible for preschool services under Part B, to discuss the appropriate services that the child may receive;
- Procedures must occur to review the child's program options for the period from the child's third birthday through the remainder of the school year; and
- A transition plan must be established.

Q. Must a state submit a plan for approval under Part C? How often does it have to be submitted?

A. A state must have on file an application to the Secretary designating a number of things including:

- Information and assurances that:
  - the state-wide system of early intervention services required in Part C is in effect; and
  - a state policy is in effect which ensures that appropriate early intervention services are available to all infants and toddlers with disabilities in the state and their families, including Indian infants and toddlers with disabilities and their families residing on a reservation geographically located in the state.
- A designation of the lead agency in the state that will be responsible for the administration of Part C funds;
- A designation of an individual or entity responsible for assigning financial responsibility among appropriate agencies;
- Information demonstrating to the Secretary's satisfaction that the state has in effect the state-wide system;
- A description of services to be provided to infants and toddlers with disabilities and their families through the system;
- A description of such services, if the state provides services to at-risk infants and toddlers through the system;
- A description of the uses for which funds will be expended in accordance with this part;
- A description of the procedure used to ensure that resources are made available under this part for all geographic areas within the state; and
- A description of state policies and procedures which ensure that, prior to the adoption by the state of any other policy or procedure, there are public hearings, adequate notice of the hearings, and an opportunity for comment available to the general public, including individuals with disabilities and parents of infants and toddlers with disabilities.

The Secretary may not disapprove an application unless the Secretary determines, after notice and opportunity for a hearing, that the application fails to comply with the requirements of Part C.

If a state has on file with the Secretary a policy, procedure, or assurance that demonstrates that the state meets a requirement of Part C, including any policy or procedure filed under part H (as in effect before July 1, 1998), the Secretary shall consider the state to have met the requirement for purposes of receiving a grant.

An application submitted by a state shall remain in effect until the state submits to the Secretary such modifications as the state determines necessary. This shall apply to a modification of an application to the same extent and in the same manner as it applies to the original application.

The Secretary may require a state to modify its application, but only to the extent necessary to ensure the state's compliance with Part C if:

- An amendment is made to IDEA or a Federal regulation issued under IDEA;
- A new interpretation of IDEA is made by a Federal court or the state's highest court; or
- An official finding of noncompliance with Federal law or regulations is made with respect to the state.

Q. What is included in the statewide system under Part C?

(See sections of this document for some parallel Part B requirements.)

A. Each statewide system must include the following 16 components:

- A definition of developmental delay;
- A state policy that is in effect which ensures that appropriate early intervention services are available to all infants and toddlers with disabilities and their families;
- Provision of multidisciplinary evaluation and family-directed identification of the needs of the family;
- Provision of an IFSP, including service coordinator;
- A child find system;
- A public awareness program;
- A central directory;
- A comprehensive system of personnel development;
- Establishment and maintenance of personnel standards;
- A single line of responsibility (lead agency) determined by the Governor;
- A contracting policy;
- A procedure for reimbursement of Part C funds;
- Procedural safeguards;
- A data system;
- A state interagency coordinating system; and
- Policies and procedures ensuring the provision of services in the natural environment to the maximum extent appropriate.

Q. What procedural safeguards are required under Part C?

A. The following procedural safeguards are required under Part C:

- The timely administrative resolution of complaints by a parent. Any party aggrieved by the findings and decision regarding an administrative complaint shall have the right to bring a civil action in any state or district court of the United States without regard to the amount in controversy. In any action brought under this paragraph, the court shall receive the records of the administrative proceedings, shall hear additional evidence at the request of a party, and base its decision on the preponderance of the evidence;
- The right to confidentiality of personally identifiable information, including the right of parents to written notice of and written consent to the exchange of such information among agencies, consistent with Federal and state law;
- The right of the parents to determine whether they, their infant or toddler, or other family members will accept or decline any early intervention service under this part in accordance with state law, without jeopardizing other early intervention services under this part;
- The opportunity for parents to examine records relating to assessment, screening, eligibility determinations, and the development and implementation of the IFSP;
- Procedures to protect the rights of the infant or toddler whenever the parents of the infant or toddler are not known or cannot be found, or the infant or toddler is a ward of the state, including the assignment of an individual (who shall not be an employee of any state agency, and who shall not be

any person, or any employee of a person, providing early intervention services to the infant or toddler or to any family member of the infant or toddler) to act as a surrogate for the parents;

- Written prior notice to the parents of the infant or toddler with a disability whenever the state agency or service provider proposes to initiate or change or refuses to initiate or change the identification, evaluation, or placement of the infant or toddler, or the provision of appropriate early intervention services to the infant or toddler;
- Procedures designed to ensure that the notice required fully informs the parents, in the parents' native language, unless it clearly is not feasible to do so, of all procedures available;
- The right of parents to use mediation in accordance with section 615(e) of P.L. 105-17, except that:
  - any reference in the section to an SEA agency shall be considered to be a reference to a state's lead agency established or designated under section 635(a)(10);
  - any reference in the section to an LEA shall be considered to be a reference to a local service provider or the state's lead agency; and
  - any reference in the section to the provision of FAPE to children with disabilities shall be considered to be a reference to the provision of appropriate early intervention services to infants and toddlers with disabilities.

Q. What happens during the time a dispute is being resolved?

A. During the pendency of any proceeding or action involving a complaint by the parents, unless the state agency and the parents otherwise agree, the infant or toddler shall continue to receive the appropriate early intervention services currently being provided or, if applying for initial services, shall receive the services not in dispute.

Q. How can Part C funds be used?

A. In addition to using funds to maintain and implement the statewide system, a state may use such funds:

- For direct early intervention services for infants and toddlers and their families that are not otherwise funded through other public or private sources;
- To expand and improve services for infants and toddlers and their families that are otherwise available;
- To provide a FAPE, in accordance with Part B, to children with disabilities from their third birthday to the beginning of the following school year; and
- In any state that does not provide services for at-risk infants and toddlers, to strengthen the state-wide system by initiating, expanding, or improving collaborative efforts related to at-risk infants and toddlers, including establishing linkages with appropriate public or private community-based organizations, services, and personnel for the purposes of:
  - identifying and evaluating at-risk infants and toddlers;
  - making referrals of the infants and toddlers identified and evaluated; and
  - conducting periodic follow-up on each referral to determine if the status of the infant or toddler involved has changed with respect to the eligibility of the infant or toddler for services under Part C.

Part C funds cannot be commingled with state funds; and can be used so as to supplement the level of state and local funds expended for infants and toddlers and their families and in no case to supplant those state and local funds.

Q. What does "payor of last resort" mean as it relates to Part C funds?

A. Funds provided under Part C may not be used to satisfy a financial commitment for services that would have been paid for from another public or private source, including any medical program administered by the Secretary of Defense, but for the enactment of Part C, except that whenever considered necessary to prevent a delay in the receipt of appropriate early intervention services by an infant, toddler, or family in a

Source: *IDEA 1997: Let's Make It Work,* 1999, Reston, VA: The Council For Exceptional Children

timely fashion. Funds provided under Part C may be used to pay the provider of services pending reimbursement from the agency that has ultimate responsibility for the payment.

Further, nothing in Part C can be construed to permit the state to reduce medical or other assistance available or to alter eligibility under Title V of the Social Security Act (relating to maternal and child health) or Title XIX of the Social Security Act (relating to Medicaid for infants or toddlers with disabilities) within the state.

Q. Do these payor of last resort requirements apply to CHAMPUS?

A. Yes, as noted above they apply to any medical program administered by the Secretary of Defense.

Q. What is the role of the State Interagency Coordinating Council (ICC)?

A. The ICC, appointed by the Governor, must include members as designated in the federal statute. Overall, 20% of the members must be service providers and 20% must be parents of children with disabilities, ages 12 or younger, including one parent who must have a child with a disability age 6 or younger.

The ICC advises and assists the lead agency in the performance of their responsibilities under Part C, particularly the identification of the sources of fiscal and other support for services for early intervention programs, assignment of financial responsibility to the appropriate agency, and the promotion of the interagency agreements. The Council also:

- Advises and assists the lead agency in the preparation of applications and amendments;
- Advises and assists the SEA regarding the transition of toddlers with disabilities to preschool and other appropriate services; and
- Prepares and submits an annual report to the Governor and to the Secretary on the status of early intervention programs for infants and toddlers with disabilities and their families operated within the state.

In addition, the Council may advise and assist the lead agency and the SEA regarding the provision of appropriate services for children from birth through age 5. The Council may advise appropriate agencies in the state with respect to the integration of services for infants and toddlers and at-risk infants and toddlers and their families, regardless of whether at-risk infants and toddlers are eligible for early intervention services in the state.

Q. What is the role of the Federal Interagency Coordinator Council (FICC)?

A. The FICC is established to:

- Minimize duplication of programs and activities across Federal, state, and local agencies, relating to:
    - early intervention services for infants and toddlers (including at-risk infants and toddlers) and their families; and
    - preschool or other appropriate services;
- Ensure the effective coordination of Federal early intervention and preschool programs and policies across Federal agencies;
- Coordinate the provision of Federal technical assistance and support activities to states;
- Identify gaps in Federal agency programs and services; and
- Identify barriers to Federal interagency cooperation.

The Council's membership is designated in the statute, and 20% of the members must be parents of children with disabilities age 12 or under, including at least one parent whose child is under the age of 6 years.

Source: *IDEA 1997: Let's Make It Work,* 1999, Reston, VA: The Council For Exceptional Children 33

Q. What are the functions of the Council?

A. The Council's functions are to:

- Advise and assist the Secretary of Education, the Secretary of Health and Human Services, the Secretary of Defense, the Secretary of the Interior, the Secretary of Agriculture, and the Commissioner of Social Security in the performance of their responsibilities related to serving children from birth through age 5 who are eligible for services under Part C or under Part B;
- Conduct policy analyses of Federal programs related to the provision of early intervention services and special educational and related services to infants and toddlers and their families, and preschool children, in order to determine areas of conflict, overlap, duplication, or inappropriate omission;
- Identify strategies to address issues described above;
- Develop and recommend joint policy memoranda concerning effective interagency collaboration, including modifications to regulations, and the elimination of barriers to interagency programs and activities;
- Coordinate technical assistance and disseminate information on best practices, effective program coordination strategies, and recommendations for improved early intervention programming for infants and toddlers and their families and preschool children; and
- Facilitate activities in support of states' interagency coordination efforts.

Section 8 – Procedural Safeguards

Q. Under what conditions must "written prior notice" to the child's parents be given?

A. Notice must be given whenever an agency:

- Proposes to initiate or change; or
- Refuses to initiate or change the identification, evaluation, or educational placement of the child, or the provision of a FAPE to the child. The notice must be written in an understandable language.

This notice must include:

- A description of the action proposed or refused by the agency;
- An explanation of why the agency proposes or refuses to take action;
- A description of any other options that the agency considered and the reasons why those options were rejected;
- A description of each evaluation procedure, test, record, or report the agency used as a basis for the proposed or refused action;
- A description of any other factors that are relevant to the agency's proposal or refusal;
- A statement that the parents of a child with a disability have protection under the procedural safeguards and, if the notice is not an initial referral for evaluation, the means by which a copy of a description of the procedural safeguards can be obtained; and
- Sources for parents to contact to obtain assistance in understanding the provisions of this part.

Q. What is the "procedural safeguards notice" and is it different from the "prior written notice"?

A. Prior written notice is discussed above. The "procedural safeguards notice" is a description of "parent rights" under IDEA, and must be given to the parents of a child with a disability, at a minimum:

- Upon initial referral for evaluation;
- Upon each notification of an IEP meeting;
- Upon reevaluation of the child; and
- Upon receipt of a request for a due process hearing.

The "procedural safeguards notice" must include a full explanation of the procedural safeguards written in an understandable language relating to:

- Independent educational evaluation;
- Prior written notice;
- Parental consent;
- Access to educational records;
- Opportunity to present complaints to initiate due process hearings;
- The child's placement during pendency of due process proceedings:
- Procedures for students who are subject to placement in an interim alternative educational setting;
- Requirements for unilateral placement by parents of children in private schools at public expense;
- Mediation;
- Due process hearings, including requirements for disclosure of evaluation results and recommendations;
- State-level appeals (If applicable in that state)
- Civil actions;
- Attorneys' fees; and
- State complaint procedures.

Q. Are there any additional requirements related to written prior notice and procedural safeguards notice?

A. Yes. Both must be written in language understandable to the general public and provided in the native language of the parent or other mode of communication used by the parent, unless it is clearly not feasible to do so.

If the native language or other mode of communication of the parent is not a written language, the public agency shall take steps to ensure:

- That the notice is translated orally or by other means to the parent in his or her native language or other mode of communication;
- That the parent understands the content of the notice; and
- That there is written evidence that the requirements have been met.

Q. On what basis can a parent or public agency request a due process hearing?

A. A hearing may be initiated on any matter relating to identification, evaluation, educational placement, or the provision of FAPE.

Q. If a parent requests a hearing, are there additional responsibilities for a public agency?

A. The public agency shall inform the parents of:

- The availability of mediation; and
- Any free or low-cost legal and other relevant services available in the area.

Q. What are the parental notice requirements prior to requesting a due process hearing by a parent?

A. The public agency must have procedures that require the parent of a child with a disability or the attorney representing the child, to provide notice (which must remain confidential) to the public agency in a request for a hearing. The required notice must include:

- The name of the child;
- The address of the residence of the child;
- The name of the school the child is attending;
- A description of the nature of the problem of the child relating to the proposed or refused initiation or change including facts relating to the problem; and
- A proposed resolution of the problem to the extent known and available to the parents at the time.

Each SEA shall develop a model form to assist parents in filing a request for a due process hearing that includes the information required above.

A public agency may not deny or delay a parent's right to a due process hearing for failure to provide the notice required.

Q. Who conducts the due process hearing?

A. Whenever a complaint is received, the parents involved have an opportunity for an impartial due process hearing which shall be conducted by the SEA or by the LEA, as determined by state law or by the SEA. A hearing may not be conducted by an employee of the SEA or LEA who is involved in the education or care of the child.

Q. What are the "impartiality" requirements for a hearing officer?

A. A hearing may not be conducted by:

- A person who is an employee of the state agency or the LEA that is involved in the education or care of the child; or
- Any person having a personal or professional interest that would conflict with his or her objectivity in the hearing.

A person who otherwise qualifies to conduct a hearing is not an employee of the agency solely because he or she is paid by the agency to serve as a hearing officer.

Each public agency shall keep a list of persons who serve as hearing officers. The list must include a statement of the qualifications of each of those persons.

Q. What are the rights of both parties in a due process hearing?

A. Any party to a hearing or an appeal has the right to:

- Be accompanied and advised by counsel and by individuals with special knowledge or training with respect to the problems of children with disabilities;
- Present evidence and confront, cross-examine, and compel the attendance of witnesses;
- Prohibit the introduction of any evidence at the hearing that has not been disclosed to that party at least 5 business days before the hearing;
- Obtain a written, or, at the option of the parents, electronic, verbatim record of the hearing; and
- Obtain written, or, at the option of the parents, electronic findings of fact and decisions.

At least 5 business days prior to a hearing, each party shall disclose to all other parties all evaluations completed by that date and recommendations based on the offering party's evaluations that the party intends to use at the hearing. A hearing officer may bar any party that fails to comply from introducing the relevant evaluation or recommendation at the hearing without the consent of the other party.

Parents involved in the hearing must be given the rights to:

- Have the child who is the subject of the hearing present; and
- Open the hearing to the public.

The record of the hearing and the findings of fact and decisions must be provided at no cost to the parents.

The public agency, after deleting any personally identifiable information shall:

- Transmit the findings and decisions to the state advisory panel on special education; and
- Make those findings and decisions available to the public.

Q. Can due process hearing decisions be appealed to the SEA?

A. A decision made in a hearing is final except that any party involved in the hearing may appeal the decision under the following provisions, which may include a civil action:

- If the hearing is conducted by a public agency other than the SEA, any party aggrieved by the findings and decision in the hearing may appeal to the SEA. If there is an appeal, the SEA shall conduct an impartial review of the hearing. The official conducting the review shall:
    - examine the entire hearing record;

- ensure that the procedures at the hearing were consistent with the requirements of due process;
- seek additional evidence if necessary. If a hearing is held to receive additional evidence, all hearing rights apply;
- afford the parties an opportunity for oral or written argument, or both, at the discretion of the reviewing official;
- make an independent decision on completion of the review; and
- give a copy of the written, or, at the option of the parents, electronic findings of fact and decisions to the parties.

The SEA, after deleting any personally identifiable information, shall:

- Transmit the findings and decisions to the state advisory panel on special education; and
- Make those findings and decisions available to the public.

The decision made by the reviewing official is final unless a party brings a civil action.

Q. What are the timelines for conducting hearings and appeals?

A. The public agency shall ensure that not later than 45 days after the receipt of a request for a hearing:

- A final decision is reached in the hearing; and
- A copy of the decision is mailed to each of the parties.

The SEA shall ensure that not later than 30 days after the receipt of a request for a review:

- A final decision is reached in the review; and
- A copy of the decision is mailed to each of the parties.

A hearing or reviewing officer may grant specific extensions of time at the request of either party.

Each hearing and each review involving oral arguments must be conducted at a time and place that is reasonably convenient to the parents and child involved.

Q. What are the rights of both parties in a civil action?

A. Any party aggrieved by the findings and decision made in a hearing, on appeal to the SEA, or under the regulations on discipline, has the right to bring a civil action. The action may be brought in any state court of competent jurisdiction or in a district court of the United States without regard to the amount in controversy. The court:

- Shall receive the records of the administrative proceedings;
- Shall hear additional evidence at the request of a party; and
- Basing its decision on the preponderance of the evidence, shall grant the relief that the court determines to be appropriate.

The district courts of the United States have jurisdiction of actions brought under Section 615 (Procedural Safeguards) of the Act without regard to the amount in controversy.

Nothing in Part B of IDEA restricts or limits the rights, procedures, and remedies available under the Constitution, the Americans with Disabilities Act of 1990, Title V of the Rehabilitation Act of 1973, or other Federal laws protecting the rights of children with disabilities, except that before the filing of a civil action under these laws seeking relief that is also available under Section 615 of the IDEA, these procedures must be exhausted to the same extent as would be required had the action been brought under Section 615 of the IDEA.

Q. What happens to the child's placement during the dispute?

A. Except as provided for in the discipline procedures related to alternative educational settings, during the pendency of any administrative or judicial proceeding, unless the SEA or LEA and the parents otherwise agree, the child shall remain in the then-current educational placement of the child, or, if applying for initial admission to a public school, shall, with the consent of the parents, be placed in the public school program until all such proceedings have been completed.

If the decision of a hearing officer in a due process hearing conducted by the SEA or a state review official in an administrative appeal agrees with the child's parents that a change of placement is appropriate, that placement must be treated as an agreement between the state or local agency and the parents.

Q. Under what circumstances are attorneys' fees awarded to parents?

A. The district courts of the United States shall have jurisdiction of actions brought under Section 615 of IDEA without regard to the amount in controversy. In any action or proceeding brought under the procedural safeguards section of IDEA, the court, in its discretion, may award reasonable attorneys' fees as part of the costs to the parents of a child with a disability who is the prevailing party. Fees awarded shall be based on rates prevailing in the community in which the action or proceeding arose for the kind and quality of services furnished. No bonus or multiplier may be used in calculating the fees awarded.

Attorneys' fees may not be awarded and related costs may not be reimbursed in any action or proceeding for services performed subsequent to the time of a written offer of settlement to a parent if:

- The offer is made within the time prescribed by Rule 68 of the Federal Rules of Civil Procedure or, in the case of an administrative proceeding, at any time more than 10 days before the proceedings begins;
- The offer is not accepted within 10 days; and
- The court or administrative hearing officer finds that the relief finally obtained by the parents is not more favorable to the parents than the offer of settlement.

In addition, attorneys' fees may not be awarded relating to any meeting of the IEP team unless the meeting is convened as a result of an administrative proceeding or judicial action, or, at the discretion of the state, for a mediation that is conducted prior to the filing of a request for a due process hearing. An award of attorneys' fees and related costs may be made to a parent who is the prevailing party and who was substantially justified in rejecting the settlement offer.

The court shall reduce, accordingly, the amount of the attorneys' fees whenever the court finds that:

- The parent, during the course of the action or proceeding, unreasonably protracted the final resolution of the controversy;
- The amount of the attorneys' fees otherwise authorized to be awarded unreasonably exceeds the hourly rate prevailing in the community for similar services by attorneys of reasonably comparable skill, reputation, and experience;
- The time spent and legal services furnished were excessive considering the nature of the action or proceeding; or
- The attorney representing the parent did not provide to the school district the appropriate information in the due process complaint. However, the award may not be reduced if the court finds that the SEA or LEA unreasonably protracted the final resolution of the action or proceeding or there was a violation of procedural safeguards requirements.

Funds under Part B of the Act may not be used to pay attorneys' fees or costs of a party related to an action or proceeding under Section 615 of the Act and subpart E of this part. This does not preclude a public agency from using funds under Part B of the Act for conducting an action or proceeding under Section 615 of the Act.

Q. Who can act as a parent for the purpose of due process?

A. The term parent means:

- A natural or adoptive parent of a child;
- A guardian but not the state if the child is a ward of the state;
- A person acting in the place of a parent (such as a grandparent or stepparent with whom the child lives, or a person who is legally responsible for the child's welfare); or
- A surrogate parent who has been appointed.

Unless state law prohibits a foster parent from acting as a parent, a state may allow a foster parent to act as a parent if:

- The natural parents' authority to make educational decisions on the child's behalf has been extinguished under state law; and

The foster parent:

- Has an ongoing, long-term parental relationship with the child; and
- Is willing to make the educational decisions required of parents under the IDEA; and
- Has no interest that would conflict with the interests of the child.

Q. What are the requirements related to surrogate parents?

A. Each public agency shall ensure that the rights of a child are protected if:

- No parent can be identified;
- The public agency, after reasonable efforts, cannot discover the whereabouts of a parent; or
- The child is a ward of the state under the laws of that state.

The duty of a public agency includes the assignment of an individual to act as a surrogate for the parents. This must include a method:

- For determining whether a child needs a surrogate parent; and
- For assigning a surrogate parent to the child.

The public agency may select a surrogate parent in any way permitted under State law. The public agency shall ensure that a person selected as a surrogate:

- Is not an employee of the SEA, the LEA, or any other agency that is involved in the education or care of the child;
- Has no interest that conflicts with the interest of the child he or she represents; and
- Has knowledge and skills that ensure adequate representation of the child.

A public agency may select as a surrogate a person who is an employee of a non-public agency that only provides non-educational care for the child and who meets the above standards.

A person who otherwise qualifies to be a surrogate parent is not an employee of the agency solely because he or she is paid by the agency to serve as a surrogate parent. The surrogate parent may represent the child on all matters relating to:

- The identification, evaluation, and educational placement of the child; and

 Source: *IDEA 1997: Let's Make It Work,* 1999, Reston, VA: The Council For Exceptional Children

- The provision of FAPE to the child.

Q. What happens when a child reaches the age of majority?

A. IDEA permits, but does not require, that the state provide that when a child with a disability reaches the age of majority under state law that applies to all students (except for a child with a disability who has been determined to be incompetent under state law):

- The public agency shall provide any notice required to both the individual and the parents;
- All other rights accorded to parents under IDEA transfer to the child;
- The agency shall notify the individual and the parents of the transfer of rights; and
- All rights accorded to parents transfer to children who are incarcerated in an adult or juvenile state or local correctional institution.

If under state law, a child with a disability who has reached the age of majority under state law that applies to all children, who has not been determined to be incompetent, but who is determined not to have the ability to provide informed consent with respect to their educational program, the state shall establish procedures for appointing the parents of the child, or if the parent is not available, another appropriate individual, to represent the educational interests of the child throughout the period of eligibility of the child.

Q. If a state elects to "transfer rights" at the age of majority, can parents continue to attend IEP meetings?

A. Yes. At the discretion of the student or the public agency, the parents could attend IEP meetings as "individuals who have knowledge or special expertise regarding the child."

Q. Is consent defined under IDEA?

A. Yes. Consent means that:

- The parent has been fully informed of all information relevant to the activity for which consent is sought, in his or her native language, or other mode of communication;
- The parent understands and agrees in writing to the carrying out of the activity for which his or her consent is sought, and the consent describes that activity and lists the records (if any) that will be released and to whom; and
- The parent understands that the granting of consent is voluntary on the part of the parent and may be revoked at any time.

If a parent revokes consent, that revocation is not retroactive (i.e., it does not negate an action that has occurred after the consent was given and before the consent was revoked).

Q. What are the requirements related to parental consent?

A. In general, informed parental consent must be obtained before:

- Conducting an initial evaluation or reevaluation; and
- Initial provision of special education and related services to a child with a disability.

Consent for initial evaluation may not be construed as consent for initial placement.
Parental consent is not required before:

- Reviewing existing data as part of an evaluation or a reevaluation; or
- Administering a test or other evaluation that is administered to all children unless, before administration of that test or evaluation, consent is required of parents of all children.

If the parents of a child with a disability refuse consent for initial evaluation or a reevaluation, the agency may continue to pursue those evaluations by using the due process procedures or the mediation procedures, if appropriate, except to the extent inconsistent with state law relating to parental consent.

Informed parental consent need not be obtained for reevaluation if the public agency can demonstrate that it has taken reasonable measures to obtain that consent, and the child's parent has failed to respond. To meet the reasonable measures requirement the public agency must use procedures consistent with those required for conducting an IEP meeting without a parent in attendance.

In addition to the parental consent requirements described above, a state may require parental consent for other services and activities under IDEA if it ensures that each public agency in the state establishes and implements effective procedures to ensure that a parent's refusal to consent does not result in a failure to provide the child with FAPE.

A public agency may not use a parent's refusal to consent to one service or activity to deny the parent or child any other service, benefit, or activity of the public agency, except as required by IDEA.

Q. What are the requirements related to independent educational evaluations?

A. The parents of a child with a disability have the right to obtain an independent educational evaluation of the child, subject to the conditions outlined below:

- Each public agency shall provide to parents, upon request for an independent educational evaluation, information about where an independent educational evaluation may be obtained, and the agency criteria applicable for independent educational evaluations;
- Independent educational evaluation means an evaluation conducted by a qualified examiner who is not employed by the public agency responsible for the education of the child in question; and
- Public expense means that the public agency either pays for the full cost of the evaluation or ensures that the evaluation is otherwise provided at no cost to the parent.

A parent has the right to an independent educational evaluation at public expense if the parent disagrees with an evaluation obtained by the public agency.

If a parent requests an independent educational evaluation at public expense, the public agency must, without unnecessary delay, either:

- Initiate a due process hearing to show that its evaluation is appropriate; or
- Ensure that an independent educational evaluation is provided at public expense, unless the agency demonstrates in a due process hearing that the evaluation obtained by the parent did not meet agency criteria.

If the public agency initiates a hearing and the final decision is that the agency's evaluation is appropriate, the parent still has the right to an independent educational evaluation, but not at public expense.

If a parent requests an independent educational evaluation, the public agency may ask for the parent's reason why he or she objects to the public evaluation. However, the explanation by the parent may not be required and the public agency may not unreasonably delay either providing the independent educational evaluation at public expense or initiating a due process hearing to defend the public evaluation.

If the parent obtains an independent educational evaluation at private expense, the results of the evaluation:

- Must be considered by the public agency, if it meets agency criteria, in any decision made with respect to the provision of FAPE to the child; and
- May be presented as evidence at a due process hearing regarding that child.

Source: *IDEA 1997: Let's Make It Work,* 1999, Reston, VA: The Council For Exceptional Children

If a hearing officer requests an independent educational evaluation as part of a hearing, the cost of the evaluation must be at public expense. If an independent educational evaluation is at public expense, the criteria under which the evaluation is obtained, including the location of the evaluation and the qualifications of the examiner, must be the same as the criteria that the public agency uses when it initiates an evaluation, to the extent those criteria are consistent with the parent's right to an independent educational evaluation.

Except for the criteria described above, a public agency may not impose conditions or timelines related to obtaining an independent educational evaluation at public expense.

Q. What are the requirements related to parent participation in meetings and involvement in placement decisions?

A. The parents of a child with a disability must be afforded an opportunity to participate in meetings with respect to:

- The identification, evaluation, and educational placement of the child; and
- The provision of FAPE to the child.

Each public agency shall provide notice consistent with the notification requirements for an IEP meeting to ensure that parents of children with disabilities have the opportunity to participate in meetings described in this section.

A meeting does not include informal or unscheduled conversations involving public agency personnel and conversations on issues such as teaching methodology, lesson plans, or coordination of service provision, if those issues are not addressed in the child's IEP. A meeting also does not include preparatory activities that public agency personnel engage in to develop a proposal or response to a parent proposal that will be discussed at a later meeting.

Each public agency shall ensure that the parents of each child with a disability are members of any group that makes decisions on the educational placement of their child.

In implementing the above requirements for parent involvement in placement decisions, the public agency shall use procedures consistent with the notification requirements for an IEP meeting.

If neither parent can participate in a meeting in which a decision is to be made relating to the educational placement of their child, the public agency shall use other methods to ensure their participation, including individual or conference telephone calls, or video conferencing.

A placement decision may be made by a group without the involvement of the parents, if the public agency is unable to obtain the parents' participation in the decision. In this case, the public agency must have a record of its attempt to ensure their involvement, including information that is consistent with the requirements for conducting an IEP meeting without a parent in attendance.

The public agency shall make reasonable efforts to ensure that the parents understand, and are able to participate in, any group discussions relating to the educational placement of their child, including arranging for an interpreter for parents with deafness, or whose native language is other than English.

Comments from the Senate Committee

As we stated in the 1986 report accompanying the legislation that added the attorneys' fees provisions: "It is the committee's intent that the terms 'prevailing party' and 'reasonable' be construed consistent with the U.S. Supreme Court's decision in *Hensley v. Eckerhart*, 461 U.S. 424, 440 (1983)." In this case, the Court held that:

> the extent of a plaintiff's success is a crucial factor in determining the proper amount of an award of attorneys' fees. Where the plaintiff has failed to prevail on a claim that is distinct in all respects from his successful claims, the hours spent on the unsuccessful claim should be excluded in considering the amount of a reasonable fee. Where a lawsuit consists of related claims, a plaintiff who has won substantial relief should not have his attorney's fees reduced simply because the court did not adopt each contention raised. But where the plaintiff achieved only limited success, the district court should award only that amount of fees that is reasonable in relation to the results obtained. *Senate Report p. 26*

Section 9 - Mediation

Q. Whose responsibility is it to ensure that procedures are established and implemented to allow parties to disputes to resolve conflicts through a mediation process?

A. Under a new IDEA requirement, SEAs and LEAs must ensure that procedures are in place to provide mediation.

Q. Is a public agency required to inform parents of the availability of mediation?

A. Yes. When a due process hearing is initiated, the public agency shall inform the parents of the availability of mediation.

Q. Is mediation required?

A. No. However, SEAs or LEAs are required to offer mediation and ensure that procedures are established and implemented to allow parties to use mediation. The mediation process must be voluntary on the part of the parties, not used to deny or delay a parent's right to a due process hearing or to deny any other rights under IDEA; and be conducted by a qualified and impartial mediator trained in effective mediation techniques. Each session in the mediation process must be scheduled in a timely manner and must be held in a location that is convenient to the parties to the dispute. At a minimum, mediation must be offered anytime a due process hearing or an expedited due process hearing is requested under the discipline procedures.

Q. What determines a "qualified and impartial" mediator?

A. The U.S. Department of Education final regulations provide that the mediator may not be an employee of any LEA nor of any state agency or SEA that is providing direct services to a child who is the subject of the mediation process, and may not be a person who has a personal or professional conflict of interest. A person who otherwise qualifies as a mediator is not an employee of an LEA or stateagency solely because he or she is paid by the agency to serve as a mediator.

Q. What happens if a parent chooses not to go through the mediation process?

A. An LEA or SEA may establish procedures to require parents who choose not to use the mediation process to meet, at a time and place convenient for the parent, with a "disinterested party" - who is under contract with a parent training and information center, community parent resource center, or an appropriate alternative dispute resolution entity - who would encourage and explain the benefits of mediation.

A public agency may not deny or delay a parent's right to a due process hearing if the parent fails to participate in the meeting.

Q. Who chooses the mediator?

A. The state must maintain a list of individuals who are qualified mediators and knowledgeable in laws and regulations relating to the provision of special education and related services. When a mediator is not chosen at random, then both the parents and the agency are involved in the selection process and must agree with the individual selected.

Q. Who pays for the cost of mediation?

A. IDEA requires the state to bear the cost of mediation, including the cost of meetings with a disinterested party for those parents who choose not to use the mediation process. Part B funds reserved for state-level activities under IDEA may be used to establish and implement a mediation process, including the costs of mediators and support personnel.

Q. Must the mediation agreement be adhered to?

A. An agreement to the dispute in the mediation process must be set forth in a written agreement. Because both parties have agreed to mediation it is understood that both parties will adhere to the agreement.

Q. Can attorneys be used in mediation?

A. There is no reference in the statute or regulations to the use of attorneys.

Q. Can the results in the mediation process be used as evidence if due process or civil proceedings follow?

A. Discussions that occur during the mediation process must be confidential and may not be used as evidence in any subsequent due process hearings or civil proceedings, and the parties to the mediation process may be required to sign a confidentiality pledge prior to the commencement of the process.

Q. Can attorneys' fees be awarded for mediation?

A. Attorneys' fees may not be awarded at the discretion of the state for a mediation that is conducted prior to the filing of a request for a due process hearing. However, it should be noted that in the past, case law has allowed for the award of attorneys' fees for assistance during mediation.

Comments from the Senate Committee

The Committee believes that, in states where mediation is now offered, mediation is proving successful both with and without the use of attorneys. Thus, the Committee wishes to respect the individual state procedures with regard to attorney use in mediation, and, therefore, neither requests nor prohibits the use of attorneys in mediation. The Committee is aware that, in states where mediation is being used, litigation has been reduced, and parents and schools have resolved their differences amicably, making decisions with the child's best interest in mind. It is the Committee's strong preference that mediation become the norm for resolving disputes under IDEA. The Committee believes that the availability of mediation will ensure that far fewer conflicts will proceed to the next procedural steps, formal due process and litigation, outcomes that the Committee believes should be avoided when possible.

The Committee intends that nothing in this bill shall supersede any parental access rights under the Family Educational Rights and Privacy Act of 1974 or foreclose access to information otherwise available to the parties. Mediation parties may enter into a confidentiality pledge or agreement prior to the commencement of mediation. An example of such an agreement follows:

- The mediator, the parties, and their attorneys agree that they are all strictly prohibited from revealing to anyone, including a judge, administrative hearing officer, or arbitrator the content of any discussions which take place during the mediation process. This includes statements made, settlement proposals made or rejected, evaluations regarding the parties, their good faith, and the reasons a resolution was not achieved, if that be the case. This does not prohibit the parties from discussing information, on a need-to-know basis, with appropriate staff, professional advisors, and witnesses.

- The parties and their attorneys agree that they will not at any time, before, during, or after mediation, call the mediator or anyone associated with the mediator as a witness in any judicial, administrative, or arbitration proceeding concerning this dispute.
- The parties and their attorneys agree not to subpoena or demand the production of any records, notes, work product, or the like of the mediator in any judicial, administrative, or arbitration proceeding concerning this dispute.
- If, at a later time, either party decides to subpoena the mediator or the mediator's records, the mediator will move to quash the subpoena. The party making the demand agrees to reimburse the mediator for all expenses incurred, including attorney fees, plus the mediator's then-current hourly rate for all time taken by the matter.
- The exception to the above is that this agreement to mediate and any written agreement made and signed by the parties as a result of mediation may be used in any relevant proceeding, unless the parties agree in writing not to do so. Information which would otherwise be subject to discovery, shall not become exempt from discovery by virtue of it being disclosed during mediation. *Senate Report*, p. 27

Section 10 - Behavior and Discipline

In this section, the term "exclusion" is used to describe cessation of all educational services. The term "removal" is used to describe a change in placement such as a suspension from school, but during which some educational services must be provided.

Q. Under IDEA, when does the LEA become responsible for addressing the behavior of a child with a disability?

A. For most children with behavioral problems, there is a history of misbehavior prior to identification. If a child with a disability has a history of behavior problems that interfere with his/her learning or the learning of others, the IEP team must consider, if appropriate, positive behavior intervention strategies and supports. If the IEP team determines that such services are needed, they must be included in the IEP and must be provided. This process may include a functional behavioral assessment and the development and implementation of a behavior intervention plan.

Q. What due process protections are available under IDEA to a child who is currently not identified as qualifying for services under IDEA?

A. A parent or child may claim due process protections under IDEA if the district had reason to believe that the child had a disability that adversely affects educational performance. The district shall be assumed to have such a reason when:

- The parent of the child has expressed concern in writing (or orally if writing is not an option) to school personnel that the child is in need of special education and related services;
- The parent has requested an evaluation of the child for special education;
- When the behavior or performance of the child demonstrates a need for services that appears to be based upon the presence of a disability that adversely affects educational performance; or
- The teacher of the child or other school personnel has expressed concern about the behavior or performance of the child to the director of special education or other school personnel in accordance with the agency's established child find or special education referral system.

If a request is made for an evaluation to determine a need for special education services during the time that a child is subjected to disciplinary measures, the evaluation must be conducted in an expedited manner. Until the evaluation is completed, the child remains in the placement determined by school authorities, which may include exclusion from all educational services.

Q. Can a child with a disability be excluded from school for disciplinary reasons with no continuation of services?

A. Yes, if two conditions are met:

- The exclusion does not exceed 10 consecutive days or constitute a change in placement; and
- A child without a disability who demonstrated the same behavior would receive the same consequence.

Q. Is there a specific limit to the total number of school days in a year that a child with a disability may be removed from school for disciplinary reasons?

A. No. However, removals that constitute a change of placement require additional considerations. The provisions regarding the amount of time a child can be excluded or removed to a temporary placement for disciplinary reasons apply only if the removal constitutes a change in placement. It should be remembered that the placement of a child may be changed at any time and without time limitation given agreement between the LEA and the child's parents.

Q. What is the definition of a change in placement for disciplinary purposes?

A. A change in placement occurs when a child's placement is changed:

- Due to a series of disciplinary removals that cumulatively total more than 10 days and a pattern is present based upon factors such as the length of each removal, the amount of total time of removals, and the proximity of removals to one another; OR
- For more than 10 consecutive school days for disciplinary purposes.

Whether a pattern of removals constitutes a "change of placement" is determined on a case-by-case basis by school personnel. The decision is subject to review through due process and judicial proceedings.

Q. Do suspensions from a school bus count toward the 10 days or in the consideration of a pattern of removals?

A. The only time a bus suspension counts for these purposes is when the bus transportation is part of the child's IEP and no alternative transportation is provided by the school. The U.S. Department of Education recommends that IEP teams consider whether or not historical bus behavior problems are similar to classroom behavior problems and may thus indicate a need for bus behavior to be addressed in the IEP.

Q. Do in-school suspensions count toward the 10 days or in the consideration of a pattern of removals?

A. In-school suspension does not count if the child continues to receive the services in his/her IEP, has the opportunity to progress in the general curriculum, and continues to participate with non-disabled children to the same extent as before. If any of these three criteria are not met, in-school suspension does count toward the 10 days.

Q. How is it decided if educational services must continue during disciplinary removals from school, and what services must be provided under those circumstances?

A. The decision is based upon the following:

- If the removal does not result in a cumulative removal of more than 10 days in the school year, services do not need to be provided.
- If removals exceed a total of 10 days in a school year and are not prohibited by virtue of being a change in placement, school personnel, including the child's special education teacher, determine the services that must be provided in order to enable the child to:
    - progress in the general curriculum; and
    - achieve IEP goals.

An IEP team meeting is not required to make this determination. However, within 10 business days, the school shall convene an IEP team meeting to schedule a functional behavioral assessment; as soon as possible after completing this assessment, the IEP team shall meet again to develop and implement a behavior intervention plan.

If the child already has a behavior intervention plan at the time, the IEP team shall meet to review the plan and its implementation and modify it as necessary.

Then, if subsequent disciplinary removals occur that do not constitute a change in placement, the IEP team members review the plan and its implementation. The IEP team shall meet only if one or more of the team members believes that modifications are necessary.

- If the removal constitutes a change of placement, the placement and the services that are necessary are based, in part, on the behavior leading to the disciplinary action.

Source: *IDEA 1997: Let's Make It Work,* 1999, Reston, VA: The Council For Exceptional Children

- If the removal is due to a violation of weapon or drug policies, the IEP team selects an interim alternate educational setting (IAES) that provides:
  - opportunity to progress in the general curriculum;
  - opportunity to progress in meeting the IEP goals; and
  - services and modifications that are designed to prevent the behavior from recurring.
- If the removal is due to some other offense or misbehavior, the IEP team determines the services (including setting) that are necessary to enable the child to:
  - progress in the general curriculum; and
  - achieve IEP goals.
- If the removal is due to a hearing officer determination that maintaining the current placement is substantially likely to result in injury to the child or others, school personnel in consultation with the student's special education teacher select the IAES that the hearing officer agrees provides:
  - opportunity to progress in the general curriculum;
  - opportunity to progress in meeting the IEP goals; and
  - services and modifications that are designed to prevent the behavior from recurring.

Q. Are there limitations on the duration of placement in an Interim Alternative Educational Setting (IAES)?

A. IAES is a phrase that is used exclusively to describe interim placements made as a result of a removal for drug or weapon violations or due to a hearing officer or court ruling that maintaining the current placement would be likely to result in injury to the child or to others.

- If parents and the school agree that a proposed change of placement for disciplinary reasons is necessary, this can be achieved through the IEP process. The requirements and limitations of the IAES do not apply in this circumstance. Of course, any changes made by the IEP team would need to provide the child with all the services and protections under the Act.
- The following limitations apply to the duration of placement in an IAES:

For a weapon or drug offense that is a manifestation of the child's disability, a child may be placed by school officials in an interim alternate educational setting for no more than 45 calendar days. This time may be extended in 45 calendar day increments by a hearing officer or as a result of court order.

If the weapon or drug offense is determined not to be a manifestation of the child's disability, the student may be removed for the same number of school days that a non-disabled student would be removed, even if that exceeds 45 days. After the 10 cumulative days of allowable exclusion, the child would be provided services allowing them to:

- Progress in the general curriculum; and
- Achieve IEP goals

If a hearing officer orders a change in placement because the child's presence in the previous setting is substantially likely to result in injury to the child or others, the IAES placement is limited to 45 calendar days. The hearing officer or judge may grant an unlimited number of extensions (of no longer than 45 calendar days each) if she/he determines that the risk of injury to the child or others continues.

Q. Under what conditions may a hearing officer order a change in placement?

A. A hearing officer must rule that all of the following conditions are met before a change in placement can be ordered:

- Substantial evidence is presented by the school that maintaining the current placement of the child is substantially likely to result in injury to the child or others;
- The current placement is appropriate;

- The public agency has made reasonable efforts to minimize the risk, including supplementary aids and services; and
- The IAES chosen by school personnel who have consulted with the child's special education teacher meets all requirements.

Q. What is a manifestation determination and when is it required?

A. A manifestation determination is a review of the relationship between the child's disability and the behavior subject to the disciplinary action. If the result of the review is that the behavior was not a manifestation of the disability, the child may be disciplined in the same manner as a child without a disability, except exclusion (the cessation of all educational services) may not exceed 10 consecutive days or constitute a change in placement.

Manifestation determinations are required within 10 school days of any proposed change in placement for disciplinary reasons, including drugs, weapons, or a hearing officer's determination of risk of injury to self or others.

Q. How is a manifestation determination conducted?

A. The IEP team and other qualified personnel consider:

- Evaluation and diagnostic results;
- Relevant information supplied by the parents; and
- Observations of the child.

Based upon this information, the IEP team determines:

- If the child's IEP and placement were appropriate;
- If services and interventions on the IEP were implemented;
- That the disability did not impair the child's ability to understand the impact and consequences of the behavior; and
- That the disability did not impair the ability of the child to control the behavior.

If any of these conditions have NOT been met, the IEP team must find that the behavior WAS a manifestation of the disability.

If the IEP team finds that ALL of these conditions have been met, the IEP team may rule that the behavior was NOT a manifestation of the child's disability.

Q. What are the practical implications of the outcome of a manifestation determination?

A. The practical implications of a manifestation determination include:

- If the behavior was found to be a manifestation and did not involve weapons, drugs, or likelihood of injury to self or others (as determined by a hearing officer), the child is returned to the current placement. If there were deficiencies in the child's IEP, placement, or their implementation, the school must take immediate steps to remedy the deficiencies.

- If the behavior was found to be a manifestation and involved weapons or drugs, the IEP team determines the IAES. If there were deficiencies in the child's IEP, placement, or their implementation, the school must take immediate steps to remedy the deficiencies.

- If the behavior was found to be a manifestation and a hearing officer determines that there is a substantial likelihood of injury to self or others, school personnel in consultation with the child's special education teacher select the IAES.

- If the behavior is not a manifestation of the disability, the child may be disciplined in the same manner, as nondisabled children would be for the same offense (including removal from school). The IEP team determines services that must be provided to allow the child to progress in the general curriculum and make progress toward achieving IEP goals.

Q. What if the manifestation determination finds that the behavior is not a result of the child's disability and a parent disagrees?

A. The parent may request a due process hearing, which must be provided by the SEA or LEA. The child remains in the current setting during the pendency of the appeal unless the parent and LEA agree otherwise.

However, in the event of placement in an IAES due to a violation of weapons, illegal drugs, or a hearing officer's determination of likelihood of injury to self or others, the child remains in the IAES pending the outcome of an expedited due process hearing.

Q. May law enforcement officials be notified of criminal activity committed by a child with a disability?

A. Nothing in the 1997 Amendments to IDEA prohibits an agency from reporting criminal acts that are committed by a child with a disability to appropriate authorities, or to prevent state law enforcement and judicial authorities from exercising their responsibilities with regard to the application of Federal and state law to crimes committed by a child with a disability. An agency reporting a crime committed by a child with a disability shall ensure that copies of the special education and disciplinary records of the child are transmitted for consideration by appropriate authorities to whom it reports the crime, to the extent that the transmission is permitted by the Family Education Rights and Privacy Act.

Source: *IDEA 1997: Let's Make It Work,* 1999, Reston, VA: The Council For Exceptional Children

Section 11 - State/Local Fiscal and Management Responsibilities

To be eligible for Part B funds for any fiscal year, a state must demonstrate that it has in effect policies and procedures to ensure the requirements of IDEA, Part B, Section 612 are met. These responsibilities include 22 components.

In order to receive Part B funds from the state, an LEA must have in effect policies, procedures, and programs that are consistent with the 22 components of Section 612, plus additional provisions included in Section 613.

Most of these state and local responsibilities are addressed in other sections throughout this document with the exception of the following, which are described here.

Q. What is the central requirement of the IDEA?

A. The state must make available a FAPE to all children with disabilities residing in the state between the ages of 3 and 21, inclusive, including children with disabilities who have been suspended or expelled from school.

Q. Is there any limitation on this requirement?

A. The obligation to make a FAPE available to all children with disabilities does not apply with respect to children:

- Ages 3 through 5 and 18 through 21 in a state to the extent that its application to those children would be inconsistent with state law or practice, or the order of any court, respecting the provision of public education to children in those age ranges; and
- Ages 18 through 21 to the extent that state law does not require that special education and related services under Part B be provided to children with disabilities who, in the educational placement prior to their incarceration in an adult correctional facility:
    - who have graduated from high school with a regular diploma;
    - were not actually identified as being a child with a disability under the IDEA; or
    - did not have an IEP under Part B of IDEA who have graduated from high school with a regular diploma

Q. How does the IDEA define a child with a disability?

(Also see *Section 3: Eligibility* of this document)

A. A child with a disability is a child with mental retardation, hearing impairments (including deafness), speech or language impairments, visual impairments (including blindness), serious emotional disturbance (hereinafter referred to as "emotional disturbance"), orthopedic impairments, autism, traumatic brain injury, other health impairments, or specific learning disabilities; and who, by reason thereof, needs special education and related services. However, nothing in IDEA requires that children be classified by their disability, so long as each child who has a disability listed above, and who, by reason of that disability, needs special education and related services, is regarded as a child with a disability under Part B of IDEA.

Q. Is there an obligation to find all children who may be eligible for special education and related services?

A. All children with disabilities residing in the state, including children with disabilities attending private schools, regardless of the severity of their disabilities, and who are in need of special education and related services must be identified, located, and evaluated, and a practical method must be developed and implemented to determine which children with disabilities are currently receiving needed special education and related services. This obligation also applies to highly mobile children with disabilities, and children suspected of being a child with a disability in need of special education and related services, even though they are advancing from grade to grade.

Q. What is meant by the obligation of each SEA and LEA to educate all eligible children in the "least restrictive environment" (LRE)?

A. To the maximum extent appropriate, children with disabilities, including children in public or private institutions or other care facilities, must be educated with children who are not disabled; special classes, separate schooling, or other removal of children with disabilities from the regular educational environment shall occur only when the nature or severity of the disability of a child is such that education in regular education classes with the use of supplementary aids and services cannot be achieved satisfactorily.

Q. In order to facilitate the LRE provision, are there requirements affecting a state's distribution of state special education funds?

A. If a state uses a funding mechanism by which the state distributes state funds on the basis of the type of setting in which a child is served, the funding mechanism must not result in placements that violate the LRE requirement.

If the state does not have policies and procedures to ensure compliance with this provision, the state must provide the Secretary an assurance that it will revise the funding mechanism as soon as feasible to ensure that such mechanism does not result in such placements.

Q. What must the state do to monitor the use of suspensions and expulsions in relation to children with disabilities?

A. The SEA must examine data to determine if significant discrepancies are occurring in the rate of long-term suspensions and expulsions of children with disabilities:

- Among LEAs in the state; or
- Compared to such rates for nondisabled children within such agencies.

If such discrepancies are occurring, the SEA must review and, if appropriate, revise (or require the affected SEA or LEA to revise) its policies, procedures, and practices relating to the development and implementation of IEPs, the use of behavioral interventions, and procedural safeguards, to ensure that such policies, procedures, and practices comply with IDEA.

Q. What data will be collected on children with disabilities?

A. Each state that receives assistance under Part B, and the Secretary of the Interior, must provide data each year to the Secretary on the number of children with disabilities, by race, ethnicity, and disability category, who:

- Are receiving a FAPE;
- Are receiving early intervention services;
- Are participating in regular education;
- Are in separate classes, separate schools or facilities, or public or private residential facilities;
- For each year of age from age 14 through 21, stopped receiving special education and related services because of program completion or other reasons and the reasons why those children stopped receiving special education and related services;
- From birth through age 2, stopped receiving early intervention services because of program completion or for other reasons;

- Are removed to an interim alternative educational setting, and the acts or items precipitating those removals; and
- Are subject to long-term suspensions or expulsions.

Further, the Secretary may require other data to be collected and may permit states and the Secretary of the Interior to obtain data through sampling.

Finally, data must be provided each year on the number of infants and toddlers, by race and ethnicity, who are at risk of having substantial developmental delays, and who are receiving early intervention services under Part C.

Q. What must states do to determine if significant disproportionality based on race is occurring related to IDEA?

A. Each state and the Secretary of the Interior must provide for the collection and examination of data to determine if significant disproportionality based on race is occurring in the state with respect to:

- The identification of children as children with disabilities, and in accordance with a particular disability category; and
- The placement in particular educational settings of such children.

If it is determined that there is significant disproportionality with respect to the identification of children as children with disabilities, or the placement in particular educational settings of such children, the state or the Secretary of the Interior, as the case may be, must provide for the review and, if appropriate, revision of the policies, procedures, and practices used in such identification or placement to ensure that such policies, procedures, and practices comply with the requirements of IDEA.

Q. Is there still a Part B State Plan and if so how often does it need to be submitted for approval to the U.S. Department of Education?

A. As long as a state has on file with the Secretary policies and procedures that demonstrate that the state meets the requirements of IDEA, the state is considered to have met IDEA requirements to receive a Part B State Grant. The Secretary may require a state to modify its application, only to the extent necessary to ensure the state's compliance with Part B, in the following circumstances:

- The provisions of IDEA are amended (or the regulations developed to carry out IDEA are amended);
- There is a new interpretation of IDEA by a Federal Court or the state's highest court; or
- There is an official finding of noncompliance with Federal law or regulations.

Except for the circumstances described above, an application submitted by a state remains in effect until the state submits to the Secretary modifications the state determines are necessary. However, the state must annually describe its use of Part B funds.

The Secretary shall not make a final determination that a state is not eligible to receive a Part B grant until after providing the state:

- With reasonable notice; and
- With an opportunity for a hearing.

Q. What opportunities are there for public comment on the state policies and procedures?

A. Prior to the adoption of any policies and procedures (including any amendments to such policies and procedures), a state must ensure that there are public hearings, adequate notice of the hearings, and an opportunity for comment available to the general public, including individuals with disabilities and parents of children with disabilities.

Q. What is the state's responsibility for ensuring the requirements of Part B are met?

A. The SEA is responsible for ensuring that:

- The requirements of Part B are met; and
- All educational programs for children with disabilities in the state, including all such programs administered by any other state or local agency:
    - are under the general supervision of individuals in the state who are responsible for educational programs for children with disabilities; and
    - meet the educational standards of the SEA.

This, however, does not limit the responsibility of agencies in the state other than the SEA to provide, or pay for some or all of the costs of a FAPE for any child with a disability in the state.

A state may not reduce medical or other assistance available, or alter eligibility, under Titles V (Maternal and Child Health) and XIX (Medicaid) of the Social Security Act with respect to the provision of a free appropriate public education for children with disabilities in the state.

There is one possible exception to the SEA's responsibility. The Governor (or another individual pursuant to state law), consistent with state law, may assign to any public agency in the state the responsibility of ensuring that the requirements of Part B are met with respect to children with disabilities who are convicted as adults under state law and incarcerated in adult prisons.

Q. Who is responsible for ensuring that students with disabilities in public charter schools receive FAPE?

A. Except when State law provides otherwise, if the charter school is itself considered to be an LEA as defined under Part B, Section 300.17, then the charter school is responsible for providing FAPE. Similarly, except when State law provides otherwise, if the charter school is one school within an LEA with other schools, then the LEA is responsible for providing FAPE, and must serve those children in the same manner as it serves children with disabilities in its other schools, and provide Part B funds to those schools in the same manner as to other schools. If, however, the charter school is not considered to be an LEA or a school within an LEA, then the SEA is responsible for ensuring that children with disabilities within that school receive FAPE.

Q. Who is responsible for paying for special education and related services?

A. IDEA specifically notes the responsibility of agencies in the state other than the SEA to provide, or pay for, some or all of the costs of a FAPE for any child with a disability in the state.
In each state, the Chief Executive Officer or designee of the officer must ensure that an interagency agreement or other mechanism for interagency coordination is in effect between the SEA and any public agencies, other than education agencies, obligated under federal or state law, or assigned responsibility under state policy or interagency agreement or other interagency coordination mechanism, to provide or pay for any services that are also considered special education or related services.

This requirement can be met through:

- State statute or regulation;
- Signed agreements between respective agency officials that clearly identify the responsibilities of each agency relating to the provision of services; or
- Other appropriate written methods as determined by the Chief Executive Officer of the state or designee of the officer.

This agreement or mechanism must include provisions for all services needed to ensure the availability of FAPE, including the provision of services during the pendency of any disputes related to the agreement.

The agreement or mechanism must include the following:

- An identification of, or a method for defining, the financial responsibility of each agency for providing services that are also considered special education or related services, such as, but not limited to, assistive technology devices, assistive technology services, related services, supplementary aids and services, and transition services that are necessary to ensuring FAPE to children with disabilities within the state.

In addition, the financial responsibility of each public agency, including the state Medicaid agency and other public insurers of children with disabilities, shall precede the financial responsibility of the LEA (or the SEA responsible for developing the child's IEP).

- The conditions, terms, and procedures under which an LEA shall be reimbursed by other agencies;
- Procedures for resolving interagency disputes (including procedures under which the LEA may initiate proceedings) under the agreement or other mechanism to secure reimbursement from other agencies, or otherwise implement the provisions of the agreement or mechanism; and
- Policies and procedures for agencies to determine and identify the interagency coordination responsibilities of each agency, to promote the coordination and timely and appropriate delivery of services described in the agreement or mechanism.

Any public agency, other than an educational agency, obligated or assigned responsibility (under federal or state law or policy or the interagency agreement or mechanism) to provide or pay for a service covered in the agreement or mechanism must fulfill that obligation or responsibility either directly or through contract or other arrangement.

If a public agency other than an educational agency fails to provide or pay for the special education and related services described in this agreement or mechanism, the LEA (or SEA responsible for developing the child's IEP) must provide or pay for the services to the child. The LEA or state agency may then claim reimbursement for the services from the public agency that failed to provide or pay for such services, and that public agency must reimburse the LEA or SEA pursuant to the terms of the interagency agreement or other mechanism according to the procedures established in the agreement.

Q. May public or private insurance funds be used to pay for services required under Part B of IDEA?

A. A public agency may use funds from Medicaid or other public insurance benefits programs in which a child participates or a parent's private insurance to pay for services required under IDEA. However, the public agency may not require the parents to enroll in public insurance programs or to access their private insurance in order for their child to receive FAPE. Further, the public agency may not require parents to incur an out-of-pocket expense such as the payment of a deductible or co-pay, and may not use a child's benefits under a public insurance program if that use would:

- Decrease available lifetime coverage or any other benefit;
- Result in the family paying for services that would otherwise be covered by the public insurance program and that are required for the child outside of the time the child is in school;
- Increase premiums or lead to the discontinuation of insurance; or
- Risk loss of eligibility for home and community-based waivers, based on aggregate health-related expenditures.

In addition, a public agency may access a parent's private insurance only if it obtains informed consent each time it proposes to access that insurance, and informs the parents that their refusal to permit the agency to access their private insurance does not relieve the public agency of its responsibility to ensure that all required services are provided at no cost to the parents.

Q. Are states required to maintain fiscal effort for special education and related services? Can these requirements be waived?

(See discussion on LEA use of funds later in this section)

A. Federal Part B funds cannot be commingled with state funds. With the exception of the ability of LEAs to reduce the level of expenditures for the education of children with disabilities made by the LEA from local funds under limited circumstances, funds paid to a state under Part B will be used to supplement the level of Federal, state, and local funds (including funds that are not under the direct control of SEAs or LEAs) expended for special education and related services provided to children with disabilities, and in no case to supplant such funds. The exception to this is when the state provides clear and convincing evidence that all children with disabilities have available to them a FAPE, in which case the Secretary may waive, in whole or in part, these requirements if the Secretary concurs with the evidence provided by the state.

The Secretary must, by regulation, establish procedures (including objective criteria and consideration of the results of compliance reviews of the state conducted by the Secretary) for determining whether to grant a waiver.

The state cannot reduce the amount of state financial support for special education and related services for children with disabilities, or otherwise make available, because of the excess costs of educating those children, below the amount of that support for the preceding fiscal year.

Q. Are there exceptions to this, and what procedures would be followed if a state does not maintain support?

A. If the state fails to maintain fiscal support, the Secretary shall reduce the allocation of funds under Part B for any fiscal year following the fiscal year in which the state fails to maintain support, by the same amount by which the state fails to meet the requirement.

The Secretary may waive this requirement for one fiscal year at a time, if the Secretary determines that:

- Granting a waiver would be equitable due to exceptional or uncontrollable circumstances, such as a natural disaster or a precipitous and unforeseen decline in the financial resources of the state; or
- The state meets the standard for a waiver (as described previously, related to the state's providing FAPE statewide). If, for any year, a state fails to meet this requirement, including any year for which the state is granted a waiver, the financial support required of the state in future years shall be the amount that would have been required in the absence of that failure and not the reduced level of the state's support.

Q. Are there requirements for LEAs to submit policies and procedures to the state? If so, how often, and are there public participation requirements?

A. As long as the LEA or state agency has on file with the SEA policies and procedures that demonstrate that the LEA, or state agency, meets the requirements included in Section 613 (a) of IDEA, the SEA must consider the LEA or state agency, to be eligible for receiving a grant under Part B.

The SEA may require an LEA to modify its application, only to the extent necessary to ensure the LEA's compliance with Part B or state law, in the following circumstances:

- The provisions of IDEA are amended (or the regulations developed to carry out IDEA are amended); or
- There is a new interpretation of IDEA by Federal or state courts; or
- There is an official finding of noncompliance with Federal or state law or regulations.

Except for the circumstances described above, an application submitted by an LEA remains in effect until it submits to the SEA any modifications the LEA determines to be necessary.

The LEA must provide the SEA with information necessary to enable the SEA to carry out its duties under Part B, including information relating to the performance of children with disabilities participating in programs carried out under Part B.

If the SEA determines that an LEA or state agency is not eligible for a grant under Part B, the SEA must notify the LEA or state agency of that determination and must provide the agency with reasonable notice and an opportunity for a hearing.

If the SEA, after reasonable notice of opportunity for a hearing, finds that an LEA or state agency that has been determined to be eligible is failing to comply with any requirements described in Section 613(a) of IDEA, the SEA must reduce or discontinue any further payments to the agency until the SEA is satisfied that the agency is complying with that requirement.

In carrying out its responsibilities under this requirement, the SEA must consider any decision made in a hearing held under the Procedural Safeguards Section of IDEA that is adverse to the LEA or state agency involved in that decision.

Any state agency or LEA in receipt of a notice as described previously must, by means of a public notice, take such measures as may be necessary to bring the pendency of an action related to this action to the attention of the public within the jurisdiction of the agency.

Regarding public notice, the LEA must make available to parents of children with disabilities and to the general public all documents relating to the eligibility of the agency under Part B.

Q. What are the requirements for the use of Part B funds for LEAs?

A. Federal Part B funds must be expended in accordance with Part B requirements and must be used only to pay the excess costs of providing special education and related services to children with disabilities. These funds:

- Must be used to supplement state, local, and other Federal funds and not to supplant such funds; and
- Cannot be used, except as described below, to reduce the level of expenditures for the education of children with disabilities made by the LEA from local funds below the level of those expenditures for the preceding fiscal year.

Q. Are there any exceptions to these requirements?

A. Yes. An LEA may reduce the level of expenditures where such reduction is attributable to:

- The voluntary departure, by retirement or otherwise, or departure for just cause, of special education personnel;
- A decrease in the enrollment of children with disabilities;
- The termination of the obligation of the agency, consistent with Part B, to provide a program of special education to a particular child with a disability that is an exceptionally costly program, as determined by the SEA, because the child:
  - has left the jurisdiction of the agency;
  - has reached the age at which the obligation of the agency to provide a FAPE to the child has terminated; or
  - no longer needs such program of special education; or
- The termination of costly expenditures for long-term purchases, such as the acquisition of equipment or the construction of school facilities.

There is an additional exception to these local fiscal requirements. For any fiscal year for which amounts appropriated for Part B exceed $4,100,000,000, an LEA may treat as local funds, for these purposes, up to 20% of the amount of funds it receives under Part B that exceeds the amount it received under Part B for the previous fiscal year.

However, if an SEA determines that an LEA is not meeting the requirements of Part B, the SEA may prohibit the LEA from treating funds received under Part B as local funds for any fiscal year, only if it is authorized to do so by the state constitution or a state statute.

Q. May an LEA use funds received under Part B to carry out a schoolwide program under Section 1114 of the Elementary and Secondary Education Act (ESEA)?

A. Yes. However, the amount used in any schoolwide program may not exceed the amount received by the LEA under Part B in that fiscal year for the students with disabilities in that school. It should be noted that while the funds do not need to be used consistent with the requirements of Part B, all other Part B requirements must be met, including ensuring that children with disabilities in schoolwide program schools receive services in accordance with a properly developed IEP, and are afforded all of the rights and services guaranteed to children with disabilities under the IDEA.

Q. May services and aids for children with disabilities that are paid for using Part B funds benefit nondisabled children?

A. Yes. Aids and services in accordance with the IEP of a child with a disability that are provided in a regular class or other education related setting may also benefit nondisabled students.

Q. May an LEA use Part B funds to implement a coordinated service system to improve results for children with disabilities and their families, and if so, may this system be coordinated with coordinated services projects authorized under title XI of the Elementary and Secondary Education Act?

A. Yes, up to 5% of the amount the LEA receives under this act may be used in combination with other funds, which must include amounts other than education funds, to implement a coordinated service system. Activities may include improving the effectiveness and efficiency of service delivery, service coordination and case management, developing and implementing interagency financing strategies, and interagency personnel development. When Part B funds are used to implement a coordinated service system in the same schools where coordinated services projects authorized under title XI of the ESEA are implemented, the Part B funds should be used in accordance with the provisions of that title.

Q. Can Part B funds be used to design, implement, and evaluate a school-based improvement plan?

A. Yes, but there are extensive requirements governing the use of Part B funds for such purposes. Interested readers should consult the regulations, at 300.245-250.

Q. Are there other funds available to LEAs for capacity building and improvement of services?

A. In fiscal years in which the percentage increase in the state's allocation under IDEA exceeds the rate of inflation, states shall reserve funds to make subgrants to LEAs, to assist them in providing direct services and in making systemic change to improve results for children with disabilities in the following ways: through direct services; addressing needs identified in the State's Improvement Plan; adopting promising practices; establishing, expanding, or implementing interagency agreements; and increasing cooperative problem-solving between parents and school personnel.

Section 12 - Private School Placements

The law makes provision for three situations in which private placements of children with disabilities occur:

Voluntary parent placement: where parents place a child in a private school, because of their preference for private school education, for reasons not generally related to special education needs.

Agency placement: When a public agency, in order to meet the requirements of a FAPE, places a child in a private school or facility.

Unilateral parent placement: When parents place a child in a private school, for the purpose of providing special education and related services to their child, without the consent of or referral by a public agency.

Voluntary Parent Placement

Q. Do the Child Find requirements apply to children with disabilities who are enrolled voluntarily by their parents in private schools?

A. Yes. The requirements relating to Child Find apply to children with disabilities in the state who are enrolled in private, including religious schools. This requirement states that all children with disabilities residing in the state, including children with disabilities attending private schools, regardless of the severity of their disabilities, and who are in need of special education and related services, must be identified, located, and evaluated. The LEA must consult with the private school personnel regarding child find activities.

Q. What must be made available to children with disabilities whose parents have enrolled them in private schools?

A. To the extent consistent with the number and location of these children in the state, provisions must be made for the participation in the Part B program of children with disabilities whose parents have enrolled them in private schools.

Q. How is "participation" determined?

A. Individual children with disabilities whose parents have enrolled them in private schools do not have rights to special education and related services. However, the entire population of such children as a group have the right to services based on the following:

- Amounts expended for the provision of those services by an LEA shall be equal to a proportionate amount of Federal Part B funds; and
- Such services may be provided to children with disabilities on the premises of private, including religious, schools, to the extent consistent with law.

Q. Do children with disabilities whose parents have enrolled them in private schools have an IEP?

A. No. No private school child with a disability whose parents have enrolled them in private school has an individual right to receive some or all of the special education and related services that the child would receive if enrolled in a public school. Children with disabilities who are to receive some special education and related services must have a service plan. A service plan must meet the requirements of an IEP and must be developed within a meeting with public and private school personnel as well as parents. The goals and objectives or benchmarks of the service plan need only address the areas of service to be provided.

Source: *IDEA 1997: Let's Make It Work,* 1999, Reston, VA: The Council For Exceptional Children

Agency Placement

Q. What are the basic conditions under which a public agency can place a child with a disability in a private school?

A. Children with disabilities in private schools and facilities must be provided special education and related services, in accordance with an IEP, at no cost to their parents, if such children are placed in, or referred to, such schools or facilities by a public agency. Also see *Section 6: IEP* of this document.

Q. What is the SEA's responsibility with regard to children with disabilities placed in private schools by a public agency?

A. Children so placed have all the rights they would have if served directly by the SEAs and LEAs. Children so placed must receive an education that meets the standards that apply to education provided by the SEA and LEA (including the requirements of Part B).

Unilateral Parent Placement

Q. What are the circumstances under which public agencies must pay for private unilateral placement of children with disabilities?

A. In general, LEAs are not required to pay for the cost of education, including special education and related services, of a child with a disability at a private school or facility if that agency made FAPE available to the child and the parents elected to place the child in such private school or facility. However, the public agency shall include that child in the population of children whose needs are addressed.

If the parents of a child with a disability, who previously received special education and related services under the authority of a public agency, enroll the child in a private school without the consent or referral by the public agency, a court or a hearing officer may require the agency to reimburse the parents for the cost of that enrollment if the court or hearing officer finds that the agency had not made FAPE available to the child in a timely manner prior to that enrollment and the private placement is appropriate.

Q. Are there any limitations that can be placed on the reimbursement to parents?

A. There are several situations in which the reimbursement may be reduced or denied:

- If at the most recent IEP meeting that the parents attended prior to removing the child from the public school, the parents did not inform the IEP team that they were rejecting the placement proposed by the public agency to provide a FAPE to their child, including stating their concerns and their intent to enroll their child in a private school at public expense; or
- Ten business days (including any holidays that occur on a business day) prior to the removal of the child from the private school, the parents did not give written notice to the public agency as described previously.
- If, prior to the parents' removal of the child from the public school, the public agency informed the parents, through the notice requirements in Part B, of its intent to evaluate the child (including a statement of the purpose of the evaluation that was appropriate and reasonable), but the parents did not make the child available for such evaluation; or
- Upon a judicial finding of unreasonableness with respect to actions taken by the parents.

Q. Are there protections for parents with respect to these limitations?

A. The cost of reimbursement may not be reduced or denied for the failure of the parent to provide notice if:

- The parent is illiterate and cannot write in English;

Source: *IDEA 1997: Let's Make It Work,* 1999, Reston, VA: The Council For Exceptional Children

- Compliance with the notice requirement would likely result in physical or serious emotional harm to the child;
- The school prevented the parent from providing such notice; or
- The parents had not received notice of their responsibility to provide notice to the agency.

Section 13 – Performance Goals, Indicators, And Assessments

Each State must:

- Establish goals for the performance of children with disabilities that are consistent, to the maximum extent appropriate, with other goals and standards for children established by the state;
- Establish performance indicators the state will use to assess progress toward achieving those goals that, at a minimum, address the performance of children with disabilities on assessments, drop-out rates, and graduation rates; and
- Ensure that children with disabilities are included in general state- and district-wide assessment programs, with appropriate accommodations and modifications in administration, if necessary.

Q. What about those children who cannot participate in state- and district-wide assessment programs?

A. As appropriate, the SEA or LEA must:

- Develop guidelines for the participation of children with disabilities in alternate assessments for those children who cannot participate in state- and district-wide assessment programs; and
- Develop and, beginning not later than July 1, 2000, conduct those alternate assessments.

Q. What must occur subsequent to the establishment of performance goals and indicators?

A. The following must occur:

- Every 2 years, the state will report to the Secretary and the public on the progress of the state, and of children with disabilities in the state, toward meeting the goals; and
- Based on its assessment of that progress, the state must revise its state improvement plan as may be needed to improve its performance, if the state is participating in the State Improvement Program.

Q. How shall the information resulting from state- and district-wide assessments be made available to the public?

A. The SEA shall make available to the public, and report to the public with the same frequency and in the same detail as it reports on the assessment of nondisabled children, the following:

- The number of children with disabilities participating in regular assessments;
- The number of those children participating in alternate assessments;
- The performance of those children on regular assessments (beginning not later than July 1, 1998) and on alternate assessments (not later than July 1, 2000), if doing so would be statistically sound and would not result in the disclosure of performance results identifiable to individual children; and
- Data relating to the performance of children with disabilities shall be disaggregated:
  - for assessments conducted after July 1, 1998; and
  - for assessments conducted before July 1, 1998, if the state is required to disaggregate such data prior to July 1, 1998.

Q. How is the determination made of accommodations needed for each child and whether each child will participate in a particular state- or district-wide assessment or in an alternate assessment?

A. A child's IEP must include a statement of any individual accommodations in the administration of state- or district-wide assessments of student achievement that are needed for the child to participate in the assessment. If the IEP team determines that the child will not participate in a particular assessment or part of an assessment, the IEP must include a statement of why the assessment is not appropriate and how the child will be assessed.

Q. For some children with disabilities, is there a distinction made between the terms "appropriate modifications in the administration of assessments" and "appropriate accommodations"?

A. Yes. The following statement appears in Attachment A: Analysis of Comments and Changes which accompanied the Final Regulations: *It should be noted, however, that out-of-level testing will be considered a modified administration of a test rather than an alternative test, and as such, should be reported as performance at the grade level at which the child is placed, unless such reporting would be statistically inappropriate.*

Section 14 - Personnel Development and Standards

There are a number of provisions in the IDEA Amendments of 1997 that relate to personnel development and standards. In order to determine training and standards that may be applicable to your needs, and available in your area, you need to know what sorts of training might be available and who to contact for specific information. In order to facilitate your search, this section has been divided based upon the Federal, state, or local agency most likely to have the appropriate information.

Federally Administered Personnel Preparation Activities

The questions in this section relate to programs funded by IDEA and administered by the U.S. Department of Education. Except for the State Program Improvement Grants (described under "State Administered Personnel Preparation Activities," which follows), information relating to any of these programs can best be obtained from the U.S. Department of Education (1-800-USA-LEARN).

Q. What competitively funded programs are available from the U.S. Department of Education that might be utilized for personnel preparation?

A. These programs fall under two categories: State Program Improvement Grants (description following, under "State Administered Personnel Preparation Activities"); and Coordinated Research, Personnel Preparation, Technical Assistance, Support, and Dissemination of Information. (See *Section 15: National Support Programs* (Part D) of this document).

Q. What are the overall goals of the Coordinated Research, Personnel Preparation, Technical Assistance, Support, and Dissemination of Information grants, contracts, and cooperative agreements?

A. Activities funded under this program are designed to "address educational, related services, transitional, and early intervention needs identified by SEAs in applications submitted for state program improvement grants."

Q. What activities must be funded by these programs?

A. At least 1% of the total funds must be used to fund either or both:

- Outreach and technical assistance to historically Black colleges and universities (HBCUs) and institutions of higher education with at least 25% minority enrollment; and
- Assistance for HBCUs and institutions of higher education with at least 25% minority enrollment to assist other colleges, universities, institutions, and agencies in "improving educational and transitional services for children with disabilities."

Q. What priorities of these programs relate to personnel preparation?

A. The authorized grants, contracts, and cooperative agreements that may fund personnel preparation share their purpose with two other programs. This purpose is to "provide Federal funding for coordinated research, demonstration projects, outreach, and personnel preparation activities that are linked with, and promote, systematic change; and improve early intervention, educational, and transitional results for children with disabilities." Personnel preparation under this purpose must "help address state-identified needs for qualified personnel in special education, related services, early intervention, and regular education, to work with children with disabilities; and to ensure that those personnel have the skills and knowledge, derived from practices that have been determined, through research and experience, to be successful, that are needed to serve those children."

Q. What specific personnel needs are likely to be addressed under this program?

Source: *IDEA 1997: Let's Make It Work,* 1999, Reston, VA: The Council For Exceptional Children

A. There must be activities funded to address the following personnel needs:

- Individuals appropriately trained to provide services to infants, toddlers, and students with low-incidence disabilities;
- Individuals appropriately trained to provide services to infants, toddlers, and students with high-incidence disabilities; and
- Leadership personnel whose work affects early intervention, educational, and transitional services for children with disabilities.

There must also be funding of activities of "national significance." These activities might include projects with objectives such as improving practices for inservice or preservice training of personnel or demonstrating the application of emerging knowledge to the training of personnel.

State Administered Personnel Development Activities

The questions in this section relate to programs funded by IDEA and administered by state departments of education. Some personnel development activities are required by every state receiving IDEA funds, while other activities may be supported at the state's discretion.

REQUIRED ACTIVITIES: Even though the following are administered by the states, since they are required of all states choosing to participate in IDEA, the U.S. Department of Education's Office of Special Education Programs may monitor these activities and take corrective action if a state does not comply with the guidelines.

Q. What personnel development activities are required by every state receiving IDEA funds?

A. Each state must develop and update at least every five years a Comprehensive System of Personnel Development (CSPD) "designed to ensure an adequate supply of qualified special education, general education, and related services personnel." This plan must include an analysis of state and local needs for professional development for personnel to serve children with disabilities including:

- The number of personnel providing special education and related services; and
- Relevant information on current and anticipated personnel vacancies and shortages (including the number of individuals with temporary certification), and on the extent of certification or retraining necessary to eliminate these shortages, that is based, to the maximum extent possible, on existing assessments of personnel needs.

The CSPD requirements encompass all of the personnel preparation activities authorized under optional State Improvement Plans and under the Infant and Toddler program (Part C), so they are all listed here.

Q. What components are in a state's Comprehensive System of Personnel Development?

A. Each state, through its plan, must describe how it will:

- Prepare general and special education personnel with the content knowledge and collaborative skills needed to meet the needs of children with disabilities, including how the state will work with other states on common certification criteria;
- Prepare professionals and paraprofessionals in the area of early intervention with the content knowledge and collaborative skills needed to meet the needs of infants and toddlers with disabilities;
- Work with institutions of higher education and other organizations that (on both a pre-service and an in-service basis) prepare personnel who work with children with disabilities to ensure that those institutions and organizations develop the capacity to support quality professional development programs that meet state and local needs;

- Work to develop collaborative agreements with other states for the joint support and development of programs to prepare personnel for which there is not sufficient demand within a single state to justify support or development of a program of preparation;
- Work in collaboration with other states, particularly neighboring states, to address the lack of uniformity and reciprocity in credentialing of teachers and other personnel;
- Enhance the ability of teachers and others to use strategies, such as behavioral interventions, to address the conduct of children with disabilities that impedes the learning of children with disabilities and others;
- Acquire and disseminate, to teachers, administrators, school board members, and related services personnel, significant knowledge derived from educational research and other sources, and how the state will, if appropriate, adopt promising practices, materials, and technology;
- Recruit, prepare, and retain qualified personnel, including personnel with disabilities and personnel from groups that are under-represented in the fields of regular education, special education, and related services;
- Insure that the plan is integrated, to the maximum extent possible, with other professional development plans and activities, including plans and activities developed and carried out under other Federal and State laws that address personnel recruitment and training; and
- Provide for the joint training of parents and special education, related services, and general education personnel.

Additional options relating to early intervention include providing:

- Efforts to recruit and retain early education service providers;
- Efforts to prepare fully and appropriately qualified early intervention providers;
- Activities to train early intervention personnel to work in rural or inner city areas;
- Training for personnel to coordinate transition services for infants and toddlers from an early intervention program to other appropriate services; and
- Training of primary referral sources respecting the basic components of early intervention services available in the state.

Q. What is meant by the phrase "qualified personnel"?

A. Personnel who meet SEA-approved or SEA- recognized certification, licensing, registration, or other requirements that apply to the area in which the individuals are providing special education or related services.

Q. Are there any guidelines to assist states in developing personnel standards?

A. Yes. The SEA must ensure that standards are based on the highest requirements in the state for, and consistent with any state-approved or state-recognized certification, licensing, registration, or other comparable requirements that apply to the profession or discipline in which the individual is providing services. If standards are not based on the highest entry level requirements in the state for a particular profession or discipline, the SEA must take steps to require retraining or hiring of personnel that meet the highest requirements in the state.

In addition, SEAs may allow paraprofessionals and assistants who are appropriately trained and supervised (according to state law, regulation, or policy) to assist in provision of special education and related services.

Q. What are the highest requirements in the state applicable to a specific profession or discipline?

A. The highest requirement is the highest entry-level academic degree needed for any state-approved or -recognized certification, licensing, registration, or other requirements that apply to that profession or discipline. However, there is no requirement that the state establish a particular training standard for personnel who provide special education and related services. A state with only one entry-level academic degree for employment of personnel in a specific profession or discipline may modify that standard as necessary to ensure the provision of services to all children with disabilities in the state.

Q. Must personnel categories follow traditional categories of the professions or disciplines?

A. No. States have the flexibility to establish new occupational categories and to revise or expand those categories as needed. However, occupational categories must have a scope of responsibility and degree of supervision.

Q. What if there are not enough qualified personnel?

A. A state may adopt a policy allowing LEAs, in an area of the state where there is a shortage of qualified personnel, to employ "the most qualified individuals available who are making satisfactory progress toward completing applicable course work necessary" to meet the state's standards within three years. However, the state must have a mechanism for serving children with disabilities if instructional needs exceed available personnel who meet appropriate professional requirements in the state for a specific profession or discipline.

OPTIONAL ACTIVITIES: Each state may use up to 25% of their Part B grant (with adjustments for inflation) for state-level activities. There are a number of ways states are authorized to use these funds, some of which involve personnel preparation. You will need to check with your state department of education in order to find out if your state is supporting personnel preparation activities under any of these authorities.

Q. What IDEA-funded professional development activities might your state offer?

A. From monies set aside for administration and other state activities in Parts B and C, the state may fund:

- "Support and direct services, including technical assistance and personnel development and training";
- Activities "to assist local education agencies in meeting personnel shortages"; and
- Activities to "support implementation of the State Improvement Plan" (see previous section, Federally Administered Activities).

Q. Are there competitive grants for which states may apply and which they may use for personnel preparation?

A. Yes. States may apply for Part D funds under the Part D State Program Improvement Grants for Children with Disabilities. The purpose of the grants is to *assist state educational agencies and their partners in reforming and improving their systems for providing educational, early intervention, and transitional services, including their systems for professional development, technical assistance, and dissemination of knowledge about best practices, to improve results for children with disabilities.*

Each state, in their plan submitted for consideration, must describe the strategies the state will use to *address the identified needs for inservice and preservice preparation to ensure that all personnel who work with children with disabilities (including both professional and paraprofessional personnel who provide special education, general education, related services, or early intervention services) have the skills and knowledge necessary to meet the needs of children with disabilities,* including a description of how the state will:

- Prepare general and special educators with the necessary content knowledge and collaborative skills, including professionals and paraprofessionals in the area of early intervention;
- Work with entities that prepare preservice and inservice personnel to develop their capacities to support quality programs meeting state and local needs;
- Recruit, prepare, and retain qualified personnel, including personnel from underrepresented populations;

- Enhance the abilities of teachers to address behavior on the part of children with disabilities that impedes the learning of children with disabilities and others;
- Acquire and disseminate "significant knowledge" to teachers, administrators, school board members, and related services personnel;
- Integrate its personnel preparation activities with other professional development plans and activities;
- Endeavor to develop common certification criteria with other states, and to address reciprocity agreements for credentialing with neighboring states;
- Collaborate with other states to develop personnel preparation programs for which the individual states do not have sufficient demand; and
- Provide joint training for parents, special education personnel, general educators, and related services personnel.

Although states must apply for these grants, it appears that Congress intends to fund this program sufficiently for all states (including the District of Columbia, Puerto Rico, and outlying areas) to receive funding if they submit a satisfactory plan.

Locally Administered Personnel Preparation Activities

The questions in this section relate to programs funded by IDEA and administered by LEAs.

Q. Under what circumstances may Part B federal funds be used by LEAs for training?

A. LEAs may use Part B funds for personnel training under three authorities: general Part B funds, coordinated services system funds, or local capacity-building and improvement funds.

General Part B funds. General Part B funds may be used for personnel preparation as long as such training is an excess cost of providing special education and related services to children with disabilities. Within the provisions of this part of IDEA, assistive technology training for a child, their family, educators, and individuals who are substantially involved in the major life functions of the child is explicitly mentioned as allowable.

Coordinated services system. LEAs may use up to 5% of their Part B funds to "develop and implement a coordinated services system designed to improve results for children and families, including children and families with disabilities." Four authorized activities are "interagency personnel development for individuals working in coordinated services."

Local capacity-building and improvement. Under certain conditions, states may offer (from their Part B funds) subgrants to LEAs for local capacity-building. One of the authorized activities is to support state efforts identified in the State Improvement Plan (an optional plan states may develop and submit for consideration of Federal funding). The training activities authorized in state improvement plans are among those listed above under "required activities."

Q. Are all LEAs authorized to carry out these activities?

A. No. LEAs are not eligible to receive any IDEA funds unless they meet certain criteria to the satisfaction of the SEA. Further, in order to qualify for local capacity-building subgrants, LEAs must demonstrate to the state that:

- All personnel are appropriately and adequately trained consistent with state guidelines; and
- The LEA contributes to and uses the state Comprehensive System of Personnel Development.

Q. How may Part C funds be used locally for personnel development?

A. The Infants and Toddlers program is under the supervision of the state, therefore there are no locally administered personnel preparation activities. Such activities are the responsibility of any state receiving Part C funds under their CSPD.

Q. How may Part D funds be used locally for personnel development?

A. Programs funded under Part D, National Activities to Improve Education of Children with Disabilities, are supervised by the U.S. Department of Education. Although the grants under Subpart 1, State Improvement Grants for Children with Disabilities, are awarded to states, states must establish contractual partnerships with LEAs. Two of the authorized activities relate directly to personnel preparation. See the previous section on State Administered Activities.

Comments from the Senate Committee

Under the current program, universities receive grants based on applications made to the Department of Education. These applications generally focus on preservice training for special education teachers. In many states, the greatest need for training is for inservice training for general and special education teachers, and for preservice training in addressing the special instructional needs of children with disabilities, including their integration in general education classes, for future general education personnel. The Committee believes that, by targeting State Program Improvement Grant funds as it has, appropriate training for teachers addressing the learning needs of children with disabilities, especially general education teachers in early grades, will help reduce inappropriate referrals to special education of children who are learning disabled and improve results for children with disabilities served by both general and special education personnel. Instead of learning from a teacher whose abilities cannot properly meet the child's particular needs, children who are learning disabled will have been taught in a manner that they can understand from teachers whose training permitted them to understand that child's learning style. *Senate Report*, pp. 37-39

Section 15 - National Support Programs (Part D)

The Individuals with Disabilities Education Act Amendments of 1997, P.L. 105-17, replaced the 14 support programs that were under Parts C-G with a new Part D, National Activities to Improve Education of Children with Disabilities. There are five authorized line items under this part: State Program Improvement Grants; Research and Innovation; Personnel Preparation; Coordinated Technical Assistance, Support, and Dissemination of Information; and Technology Development, Demonstration and Utilization, and Media Services.

The new Part D programs, whose precursors were initiated in the Eisenhower years, have provided the critical infrastructure in such areas as research, professional preparation, technical assistance, technology and support, and dissemination of information that make an effective early intervention and special education program a reality for each child. The problems children, families, and teachers face are increasingly complex. The strategies of yesterday are not adequate to educate children who live and grow in increasingly turbulent times, who survive childhood diseases or accidents that formerly were fatal, or who are born very prematurely. It is essential that the training and research and development functions of IDEA Part D continue to drive improvements in all aspects of practice and keep pace with the changing priorities of IDEA. These programs provide a way to study solutions to many of the problems that have been identified, to ensure their validity before making them widespread practice, and to proactively address emerging issues.

Q. What is the focus of the new State Program Improvement Grants?

A. The purpose of this program is to assist SEAs, and others in their state, to reform and improve their systems for providing educational, early intervention, and transitional services, including their systems for professional development, technical assistance, and dissemination of knowledge about best practices, to improve results for children with disabilities. SEAs can apply for grants on a competitive basis for a period of at least one year and not more than five. Grants made to the states will not be less than $500,000 and not more than $2,000,000. A funded SEA shall not use less than 75% of the grant funds for any fiscal year to ensure there are sufficient general education, special education, and related services personnel who have the skills and knowledge necessary to meet the needs of children with disabilities and developmental goals of young children; or to work with other states on common certification criteria. If the state demonstrates it has the personnel described above, the state then must use not less than 50% for these purposes.

Q. What is the purpose of the Research and Innovation Program?

A. The purpose of this program is to produce, and advance the use of, knowledge to:

- Improve services to children with disabilities, including the practices of professionals and others involved in providing such services; and educational results to children with disabilities;
- Address the special needs of preschool-aged children and infants and toddlers with disabilities, including infants and toddlers who would be at risk of having substantial developmental delays if early intervention services were not provided to them;
- Address the specific problems of overidentification and underidentification of children with disabilities;
- Develop and implement effective strategies for addressing inappropriate behavior of students with disabilities in schools, including strategies to prevent children with emotional and behavioral problems from developing emotional disturbances that require the provision of special education and related services;
- Improve secondary and postsecondary education and transitional services for children with disabilities; and

- Address the range of special education, related services, and early intervention needs of children with disabilities who need significant levels of support to maximize their participation and learning in school and in the community.

This program contains three separate authorities: New Knowledge Production, Integration of Research and Practice, and Improving the Use of Professional Knowledge.

Q. How does the Part D Support Program address personnel preparation?

A. Part D includes the Personnel Preparation to Improve Services and Results for Children with Disabilities, which is designed to: (a) help address state-identified needs for qualified personnel in special education, related services, early intervention, and general education, to work with children with disabilities; and (b) ensure that those personnel have the skills and knowledge, derived from practices that have been determined through research and experience to be successful, that are needed to serve those children. This program contains four authorities: Low-Incidence Disabilities, Leadership Preparation, Projects of National Significance, and High-Incidence Disabilities.

Q. What is the Federal role in technical assistance and sharing of information?

A. National technical assistance, support, and dissemination activities are necessary to ensure that Parts B and C are fully implemented and to achieve quality early intervention, educational, and transitional results for children with disabilities and their families. The purpose of this program is to ensure that:

- Children with disabilities and their parents receive training and information on their rights and protections under this Act, in order to develop the skills necessary to effectively participate in planning and decision making relating to early intervention, educational, and transitional services, and in systemic-change activities.
- Parents, teachers, administrators, early intervention personnel, related services personnel, and transition personnel receive coordinated and accessible technical assistance and information to assist such persons, through systemic-change activities and other efforts, to improve early intervention, educational, and transitional services and results for children with disabilities and their families.
- On reaching the age of majority under state law, children with disabilities understand their rights and responsibilities under Part B, if the state provides for the transfer of parental rights under Section 615(m) (Transfer of Parental Rights at Age of Majority).

This program contains four authorities: Parent Training and Information (PTI) Centers, Community Parent Resource (CPR) Centers, Technical Assistance for Parent Training and Information Centers, and Coordinated Technical Assistance and Dissemination.

Q. How does IDEA maintain support in the areas of technology and media services?

A. The new Technology Development, Demonstration, and Utilization and Media Services program funds projects under both Technology and Educational Media. These efforts are designed to support activities so that:

- Appropriate technology and media are researched, developed, demonstrated, and made available in timely and accessible formats to parents, teachers, and all types of personnel providing services to children with disabilities; and
- The general welfare of deaf and hard-of-hearing individuals is promoted by:
    - bringing to such individuals an understanding and appreciation of the films and television programs that play an important part in the general and cultural advancement of hearing individuals; and
    - providing, through those films and television programs, enriched educational and cultural experiences through which deaf and hard-of-hearing individuals can better understand the realities of their environment; and

- providing wholesome and rewarding experiences that individuals who are deaf and hard-of-hearing may share.
- Federal support is designed to:
    - stimulate the development of software, interactive learning tools, and devices;
    - make information available on technology research, technology development, and educational media services and activities;
    - promote the integration of technology into curricula to improve early intervention, educational, and transitional results for children with disabilities;
    - provide incentives for the development of technology and media devices and tools that are not readily found or available because of the small size of potential markets;
    - make resources available to pay for such devices and tools and educational media services and activities;
    - promote the training of personnel to: (a) provide such devices, tools, services, and activities in a competent manner; and (b) to assist children with disabilities and their families in using such devices, tools, services, and activities; and
    - coordinate the provision of such devices, tools, services, and activities (a) among state human services programs; and (b) between such programs and private agencies.

Q. Does the reauthorized IDEA still include the Special Studies Program?

A. This program is now the Studies and Evaluations Program. It is located in Section 674 and is designed to assess progress in the implementation of the IDEA, including the effectiveness of state and local efforts. Three kinds of activities occur under this authority, including a national assessment, the Annual Report to Congress, and technical assistance to LEAs to assist them in local capacity-building and improvement projects and other local systemic improvement activities.

Summary of the Individuals with Disabilities Education Act (IDEA) Amendments of 1997 (P.L. 105-17)

I. Part A: General Provisions

Structure of the Programs. The new legislation restructures IDEA into four parts: Part A, General Provisions; Part B, Assistance for Education of All Children with Disabilities; Part C, Infants and Toddlers with Disabilities; and Part D, National Activities to Improve Education of Children with Disabilities.

Definitions. The legislation and regulations make a few important changes to definitions.

- **Child with a Disability**. The regulations clarify that a child with a disability who needs a related service, but not special education, is not considered to be a child with a disability for the purposes of IDEA unless the related service needed is defined under state law as special education rather than a related service.

- **Developmental Delay**. The definition of "child with a disability" for a child ages 3 through 9 may, at the discretion of the state and LEA, be a child who is experiencing developmental delays and who needs special education and related services, as defined by the state and measured by appropriate diagnostic instruments and procedures.

- **Other Health Impairment**. Under the "Child with a disability" definition, the regulations list a number of disabilities that may result in eligibility under the "other health impairment" category, including attention deficit disorder (ADD) and attention deficit hyperactivity disorder (ADHD). ADD and ADHD were not specifically mentioned previously.

- **Serious Emotional Disturbance**. In the section defining "child with a disability," the legislation keeps the reference to "serious emotional disturbance" but then adds "hereinafter referred to as emotional disturbance."

- **Day; Business Day; School Day**. The regulations clarify that school day means any day or partial day that children are in attendance at school for instructional purposes. Business day means Monday through Friday, except for Federal and state Holidays (unless specific holidays qualify as school days). Any time that days are mentioned and are not specified as business days or school days, they refer to calendar days.

- **Related Services**. IDEA '97 adds "orientation and mobility services" to the definition of related services.

- **Supplementary Aids and Supports**. A definition of supplementary aids and services is added and includes aids, services, and other supports that are provided in general education classes or other education-related settings to enable children with disabilities to be educated with children without disabilities to the maximum extent appropriate.

- **Transition Services**. Related services are added to list of services included under the definition of transition services.

- **Policy Letters and Regulations**. Language was added in IDEA '97 that prohibits the Secretary from establishing a rule that is required for compliance and eligibility through policy letters or other statements without following the requirements for rulemaking under the Administrative Procedures Act of Title 5, U.S. Code. The Secretary must publish quarterly, in the Federal Register, a list of correspondence from the Department of Education that describes the interpretations of IDEA or its regulations. For issues of national significance, the Secretary must widely disseminate the response to

SEAs, LEAs, parent and advocacy organizations, and other interested organizations, and not later than 1 year after, issue written guidance on the policy, question, or interpretation through such means as a policy memorandum, notice of interpretation, or notice of proposed rulemaking.

II. Part B: Assistance for Education of All Children with Disabilities

State Formula. The current child-count formula is retained until Federal appropriation reaches approximately $4.9 billion. Once the trigger has been reached, a new formula based on the population of children aged 3 through 21 (85%) and the number of children aged 3 through 21 in poverty (15%) applies to new monies in excess of the appropriation for the prior fiscal year. The legislation provides a "hold harmless" or "floor" for each state's allocation. Under the new formula, no state would receive less than the amount it received in the year before the new formula takes effect.

State Administration. For state administration and state-level activities, the law allows states to retain an amount equal to 25% of the amount the state received for fiscal year 1997 plus future increases at the lesser of the rate of inflation or Federal appropriations increases. No more than 20% of this amount can be used for administrative purposes.

LEA Capacity Building and Improvement. Whenever federal funds allocated to states increase at greater than the rate of inflation, the funds beyond inflationary increases are to be used for subgrants to LEAs for systemic change, including:
- (a) direct services for children who have been expelled and services for children in correctional facilities, children enrolled in State-operated or supported schools, and children in charter schools;
- (b) addressing needs or carrying out improvement strategies under the state's improvement plan;
- (c) adopting promising practices, materials, and technology;
- (d) establishing, expanding, or implementing interagency agreements and arrangements; and
- (e) increasing cooperative problem-solving between parents and school personnel and promoting the use of alternative dispute resolution.

State-Level Activities. State-level activities funds can be used:
- (a) for support and direct services, including technical assistance and personnel development and training;
- (b) for administrative costs of monitoring and complaint investigation, but only to the extent that those costs exceed the costs incurred for those activities during fiscal year 1985;
- (c) to establish and implement the mediation process;
- (d) to assist LEAs in meeting personnel shortages;
- (e) to develop a state improvement plan;
- (f) for activities to meet the performance goals and to support the implementation of the state improvement plan;
- (g) to supplement other amounts used to develop and implement a state-wide coordinated services system, but not to exceed 1% of the amount received by the state; and
- (h) for subgrants to LEAs for capacity building and improvement.

State Grants to Localities. Under the new legislation, state grants to localities will follow the same within-state formula as the state the formula once Federal appropriation reaches approximately $4.9 billion. There are no maximum or minimum grant levels set for local grants.

Preschool Formula. If the Federal appropriations for preschool grants is equal to or greater than the amount allocated to states for the preceding fiscal year, each state will receive the amount it received for fiscal year 1997 and any remaining funds will be distributed based on the population of children aged 3 through 5 (85%) and population of children aged 3 through 5 living in poverty (15%). No state's allocation shall be less than its allocation for the preceding year.

Preschool Subgrants to Localities. IDEA '97 requires states to award each locality 75% of the amount the agency would have received for fiscal year 1997 and additional funds based on the number of children enrolled in public and private elementary and secondary schools (85%) and the number of children living in poverty (15%).

Previous State Plans. Under the new legislation, state applications need to be submitted only once. Thereafter only amendments necessitated by official findings of compliance problems or changes in law need to be submitted.

Requirements Regarding Free and Appropriate Public Education (FAPE). The law now requires that the obligation to make FAPE available to all children with disabilities residing in the state applies to children with disabilities who have been suspended or expelled. (see following section) Along with definition changes affecting students with developmental delays, the legislation allows the governor of the state, consistent with state law, to assign to any public agency in the state the responsibility of ensuring that services are provided to children with disabilities who are convicted as adults under state law and incarcerated in adult prisons. Further provisions state that the obligation to make FAPE available to all children with disabilities does not apply with respect to children:

(a) aged 3 through 5 and 18 through 21 in a state in which it would be inconsistent with state law or practice; and

(b) aged 18 through 21 to the extent that State law does not require that special education and related services be provided to children with disabilities who were not receiving services under this part immediately prior to their incarceration in adult correctional facilities.

Additional language states that a child shall not be determined to have a disability if the determinant factor for the determination is lack of instruction in reading or math or limited English proficiency.

FAPE for Children Suspended or Expelled from School. No services need to be provided during the first 10 days of disciplinary exclusion in a school year unless such services would be provided to a child without a disability. There is no specific limit to the number of days a child may be excluded from his or her educational setting during a school year; however limitations apply if:

(a) the behavior leading to the removal is not a manifestation of the child's disability and exceeds 10 consecutive school days or otherwise constitutes a change in placement (see following section),

(a) the behavior is not a manifestation of the child's disability and such exclusions exceed 10 days in a school year, or

(b) drug or weapon offenses lead to the exclusion or there is a determination by a hearing officer that maintaining the current placement is substantially likely to result in injury to the child or others.

Change in Placement. The regulations define a disciplinary change in placement as occurring when a child is excluded for more than 10 consecutive school days or when the child has been excluded for more than 10 days in a school year and there is a pattern to those removals based on such factors as the length of the exclusions, the total time the child is excluded, or the proximity of those exclusions to one another.

Child Find. The law requires that states identify, locate, and evaluate all children with disabilities residing in the state, including children with disabilities attending private schools regardless of the severity of their disabilities. The legislation also states that nothing in the Act requires that children be classified by their disability so long as they have a listed disability and need special education and related services.

Least Restrictive Environment (LRE). Language was added requiring that if the state uses a funding mechanism that distributes state funds on the basis of the type of setting in which a child is served, the funding mechanism must not result in placements that violate the requirements of LRE. If the state does not have policies and procedures to ensure compliance, the state is required to provide the Secretary with an assurance that it will revise the funding mechanism to comply with Part B's least restrictive environment requirements.

Transition from Infant and Toddler Program to Preschool Program. IDEA now requires the LEA to participate in transition planning conferences arranged by the designated lead agency under Part C of the Act.

Graduation. The regulations clarify that graduation from high school with a regular diploma constitutes a change in placement that:
(a) terminates eligibility under IDEA,
(b) requires written prior notice to parents.

Graduation from high school with a special education diploma, a certificate of attendance, or some other level of graduation short of a regular diploma does not end eligibility under IDEA.

Regulations clarify that graduation with a regular diploma does *not* require a reevaluation.

Services for Children in Private Schools. The legislation requires that, consistent with the number and location of children with disabilities whose parents have enrolled them in private schools (without the FAPE provided by the public school being questioned), provision is made for providing special education and related services as follows: Amounts expended for the provision of these services by an LEA must be equal to a proportionate amount of available federal funds under Part B of IDEA. The services may be provided on the premises of private schools, including parochial schools to the extent consistent with law. The services must be provided by personnel meeting the same standards as personnel providing services in public schools.

Regulations require that services to be provided to individual private school students who are to receive services must be described in a "services plan." This plan is developed and put into place with the same time limitations, IEP team requirements, parent participation requirements, and requirements for the development, review and revision as apply to IEPs.

Public Reimbursement of Private Placement. IDEA '97 clarifies that LEAs are not required to pay for the cost of education, including special education and related services, of a child with a disability at a private school if the LEA made a FAPE available to the child and the parents elected to place the child in a private school.

If the parents of a child with a disability who previously received special education and related services under a public agency enroll the child in a private school without the consent or referral of the public agency, a court or hearing officer may require the agency to reimburse the parents for the cost of enrollment if it is found that the agency did not make a FAPE available to the child in a timely manner prior to that enrollment.

Limitations on Reimbursement. The cost of reimbursement may be reduced or denied if:
(a) the parents did not inform the IEP team at the most recent IEP meeting that they were rejecting the placement proposed by the public agency, including stating their concerns and their intent to enroll their child in a private school at public expense; or
(b) 10 business days prior to the removal of the child from the public school, the parents did not give written notice to the public agency.

Reimbursement may also be reduced or denied if, prior to the parents' removal of the child from the public school, the public agency informed the parents of its intent to evaluate the child, but the parents did not make the child available for the evaluation, or upon a judicial finding of unreasonableness with respect to actions of the parents.

The reimbursement cannot be reduced or denied for failure to provide notice if:
(a) the parent is illiterate and cannot write in English;
(b) compliance would likely result in physical or serious emotional harm to the child;
(c) the school prevented the parent from providing such notice; or
(d) the parents had not received notice of the notice requirement.

Interagency Agreement. IDEA '97 strengthened interagency coordination. The governor or designee must ensure that an interagency agreement or other mechanism for interagency coordination is in effect between the state education department and public agencies that are assigned responsibility to provide or pay for any services that are also considered special education or related services, including assistive technology devices and services, related services, supplementary aids and services, and transition services. The agreement must identify the financial responsibility of each agency, including the state Medicaid agency and other public insurers of children with disabilities whose financial responsibility shall precede the financial responsibility of the LEA.

Comprehensive System of Personnel Development (CSPD). Act replaces previous requirements of CSPD and requires the SEA to have in effect a CSPD that is designed to ensure an adequate supply of qualified special education, general education, and related services personnel that meets the requirements of the state improvement plan relating to personnel development.

Personnel Standards. Language governing personnel standards continues to require the SEA to establish and maintain standards to ensure personnel are appropriately and adequately prepared and trained. As in prior law, the standard must be consistent with any state-approved or recognized standards. To the extent the standards are not based on the highest requirements, the state must take steps to require retraining or hiring of personnel that meet appropriate professional requirements. Language was added that allows paraprofessionals and assistants who are appropriately trained and supervised, in accordance with state law, regulations, or written policy, to be used to assist in the provision of special education and related services. Also added is a provision that allows a state to adopt a policy that includes a requirement that LEAs make an ongoing good-faith effort to recruit and hire appropriately and adequately trained personnel, including in a geographic area where there is a shortage of such personnel, the most qualified individuals available who are making progress toward completing applicable course work necessary to meet the applicable state standards within 3 years. Regulations state that a state with only one entry-level academic degree for employment of personnel in a specific profession or discipline may modify that standard as necessary to meet their obligations under the Act.

Performance Goals and Indicators. The amended Act added language requiring a state to establish goals for the performance of children with disabilities and develop indicators to judge childrens' progress. The Act requires children with disabilities to be included in general state- and district-wide assessment programs, with appropriate accommodations where necessary. States or LEAs must develop guidelines for the participation of children with disabilities in alternate assessments for those children with disabilities who cannot participate in state- and district-wide assessment programs and must develop and conduct those alternate assessments not later than July 1, 2000.

State Supplantation of Funds. As in prior law, funds to a state cannot be commingled and cannot supplant the level of Federal, state, or local funds unless the state provides evidence that all children with disabilities have a FAPE available. However, a new provision allows states to apply for waivers to the maintenance of effort provisions for exceptional or uncontrollable circumstances, including a natural disaster or a precipitous and unforeseen decline in the financial resources of the state.

State Advisory Panel. Additional members required to be on the State Advisory Panels were added in IDEA '97, including: representatives of other state agencies involved in the financing or delivery of related services to children with disabilities; representatives of private schools and public charter schools; at least one representative of a vocational, community, or business organization concerned with the provision of transition services to children with disabilities; and representatives from the state juvenile and adult corrections agencies. A majority of the members of the panel are required to be individuals with disabilities or parents of children with disabilities.

Collection of Data on Suspension and Expulsion Rates. States are required to examine data to determine if significant discrepancies are occurring in the rate of long-term suspensions and expulsions of children with disabilities among LEAs or compared to rates for children without disabilities. If discrepancies are occurring, the SEA must review and, if appropriate, revise policies, procedures, and practices related to the development and implementation of IEPs, the use of behavioral interventions, and procedural safeguards.

Local Supplantation of Funds. New provisions allow an LEA to reduce the level of expenditures (either in total or per capita) on the education of children with disabilities when the reduction in funds is attributable to:

(a) the voluntary departure of special education personnel;

(b) a decrease in the enrollment of children with disabilities; and

(c) the termination of the obligation of the agency to provide a program of special education to a particular child with a disability that is an exceptionally costly program of special education because the child has left the jurisdiction of the agency, has reached the age at which the obligation of the agency is terminated, or no longer needs such program of special education; or

(d) the termination of costly expenditures for long-term purchases.

In addition, a new exception to the maintenance of effort requirements is added in instances where an LEA has received more Federal funds from one year to the next, and the Federal appropriation exceeds $4.1 billion. In these circumstances, the LEA may use up to 20% of the increase in Federal funds to reduce its effort of the previous year by that amount. States, however, may prevent their LEAs from reducing their effort in cases where the LEA has been cited as failing to substantially comply with the Act.

Maintenance of State and Local Financial Support. Previously, the law specified that a state could not reduce its total expenditures for special education and related services below the amount of support that it provided during the previous year. Regulations now state that there may not be reductions on either a total or per-capita basis. Regulations indicate that proceeds from public or private insurance that are utilized to provide services under IDEA are not considered to be program funds for the purposes of calculating state or local maintenance of effort.

School-Wide Programs. A new provision in IDEA '97 allows an LEA to use funds to carry out a school-wide program under section 1114 of the Elementary and Secondary Education Act of 1965, except that the amount used is limited to the number of children with disabilities in the school multiplied by the per child amount.

Services and Aids That Also Benefit Children Without Disabilities. The Act allows an LEA to use funds for the cost of special education and related services and supplementary aids and services provided in a general education class or other education-related setting to a child with a disability in accordance with the IEP of the child, even if one or more children without disabilities benefits from the services.

Integrated and Coordinated Services System. LEAs are also allowed to use not more than 5% of their IDEA funds, in combination with other amounts other than education funds, to develop and implement a coordinated services system. Funds can be spent for:

(a) improving the effectiveness and efficiency of service delivery;

(b) service coordination and case management that facilitates the linkage of IEPs and IFSPs under multiple Federal and state programs;

(c) developing and implementing interagency financing strategies for the provision of education, health, mental health, and social services, including transition services and related services; and

(d) interagency personnel development for individuals working on coordinated services. An LEA can also use funds for a coordinated services project it is carrying out under Title XI of the Elementary and Secondary Education Act of 1965.

Charter Schools. Children with disabilities attending all publicly chartered schools must be provided with all of the rights and services guaranteed under IDEA and must be served in the same manner as such children are served in non-chartered school, regardless of whether or not the charter school receives funding under Part B of IDEA.

Prior Local Plans. LEAs are not required to submit a new application if LEAs already have a prior local plan on file with the SEA. SEAs may require an LEA to modify its application if there are amendments to the Act or a new interpretation by Federal or state courts, or there is an official finding of noncompliance with Federal or state law or regulations.

Joint Establishment of Eligibility. P.L. 105-17 allows the SEA to require an LEA to establish its eligibility jointly with another LEA if the SEA determines that the LEA would not be able to establish and maintain a program of sufficient size and scope and drops the $7,500 minimum local grant requirement. An SEA may not require a charter school that is an LEA to jointly establish its eligibility unless it is explicitly permitted to do so under the state's charter school statute.

School-Based Improvement Plan. An SEA may grant authority to an LEA to select public schools to design, implement, and evaluate a school-based improvement plan for a period not to exceed 3 years. The plan must:
   (a) be designed to improve educational and transitional results for all children with disabilities and, as appropriate, for other children who attend the school;
   (b) be designed, evaluated, and as appropriate, implemented by a school-based standing panel (the panel must include parents of children with disabilities, special and general education teachers, special and general education administrators, or designees; and related services providers);
   (c) include goals and measurable indicators to assess the progress of the public school in meeting the goals; and
   (d) ensure that all children with disabilities receive the services described in their IEPs. The plan may be submitted to the LEA for approval only if a consensus with respect to any matter relating to design, implementation, or evaluation of the goals of such plan is reached by the panel.

Disciplinary Information. The Act adds provisions that allow states to require an LEA to include in the records of a child with a disability, a statement of any current or previous disciplinary action that has been taken against the child, and transmit the statement to the same extent that the disciplinary information is included in and transmitted with the records of children without disabilities. If the state adopts such a policy, and the child transfers from one school to another, the transmission of any child's records must include both the child's current IEP and any statement of current or previous disciplinary action that has been taken against the child.

Student Evaluations. IDEA '97 requires the LEA to:
   (a) use a variety of assessment tools and strategies to gather relevant functional and developmental information, including information provided by the parent, that may assist in determining
   (1) whether the child has a disability, and (2) the content of the child's IEP, including information related to enabling the child to be involved in and progress in the general education curriculum or, for preschool children, to participate in appropriate activities;
   (b) not use any single procedure for determining whether the child has a disability or determining an appropriate educational program; and
   (c) use technically sound instruments that may assess cognitive and behavioral factors in addition to physical or developmental factors.

The LEA must assess the child in all areas of suspected disability and provide assessment tools and strategies that provide relevant information that directly assists persons in determining the educational needs. The law also specifies that an informed consent from the parent of the child be obtained before the evaluation is conducted, and that the agency may continue to pursue an evaluation if the parents refuse consent by using the mediation and due process procedures, unless inconsistent with State law applicable to parent consent.

Requirements of Evaluation Tests. LEAs must ensure that tests and other evaluation materials are selected and administered so as not to be racially or culturally discriminatory and are provided and administered in the child's native language or other mode of communication, unless it is not feasible. Tests must have been validated for the specific purpose for which they are used, must be administered by trained personnel, and must be administered in accordance with any instructions provided by the producer of the test.

Source: *IDEA 1997: Let's Make It Work,* 1999, Reston, VA: The Council For Exceptional Children 81

Student Reevaluations. The statute requires that a reevaluation of a child with a disability be conducted if conditions warrant, if the child's parent or teacher requests an evaluation, but at least once every three years, in accordance with the following procedures. The legislation requires LEAs to obtain informed parental consent prior to conducting any reevaluation, except that such consent need not be obtained if the agency can demonstrate that it had taken reasonable measures to obtain such consent and the parents failed to respond. For a reevaluation, the legislation requires the IEP team and other qualified professionals to review existing evaluation data and on the basis of that review and input from the child's parents, identify:

(a) what additional data are needed to determine whether the child has or continues to have a particular category of disability;

(b) the present levels of performance and educational needs of the child;

(c) whether the child needs or continues to need special education and related services; and

(d) whether any additions or modifications to special education and related services are needed to meet performance goals and to participate, as appropriate, in the general education curriculum.

If additional data are not needed, the LEA must notify the parents of:

(a) that determination and the reasons for it, and

(b) the right of parents to request an assessment to determine if the child still has a disability.

Individualized Education Programs (IEPs). P.L. 105-17 added new IEP requirements and expanded existing requirements. The IEP is required to include:

- A statement of the child's present levels of educational performance, including how the child's disability affects the child's involvement and progress in the general education curriculum; for preschool children, as appropriate, it must describe how the disability affects the child's participation in appropriate activities;

- A statement of measurable annual goals, including benchmarks or short-term objectives related to
    (a) meeting the child's needs that result from the child's disability, to enable the child to be involved in and progress in the general education curriculum; and
    (b) meeting each of the child's other educational needs that result from the child's disability;

- A statement of the special education and related services, and supplementary aids and services to be provided to the child, or on behalf of the child, and any program modifications or support for school personnel that will be provided for the child to advance toward attaining the annual goals; to be involved and progress in the general education curriculum; to participate in extracurricular and other nonacademic activities; and to be educated and participate with other children with and without disabilities in these activities;

- An explanation of the extent, if any, to which the child will not participate with children without disabilities in the general education class and in the activities;

- A statement of any individual modifications in the administration of state- or district-wide assessments of student achievement that are needed in order for the child to participate in the assessment. If the IEP team determines that the child will not participate in the assessment or part of the assessment a statement of why that assessment is not appropriate and how the child will be assessed;

- The projected date for the beginning of the services and modifications, and their anticipated frequency, location, and duration;

- A statement of transition service needs of the child (beginning at age 14 and updated annually) that focus on the child's courses of study; a statement of needed transition services for the child, including, when appropriate, a statement of the interagency responsibilities or needed linkages (beginning at age 16 or younger); and a statement that the child has been informed of the rights that will transfer to him (or her) on reaching the age of majority under State law (beginning at least one year before the child reaching the age of majority); and

- A statement of how the child's progress toward the annual goals will be measured, and how the child's parents will be regularly informed of their child's progress at least as often as parents of children without disabilities are informed, and the extent to which the progress is sufficient to enable the child to achieve the goals by the end of the year.

IEP Team. In addition to the required participants on an IEP team under prior law, at least one regular education teacher of the child now must be a member of the team if the child is, or may be, participating in the regular educational environment. Other required participants on the IEP team include the parents of the child, at least one special education teacher of the child, a representative of the public agency, and an individual who can interpret the instructional implications of evaluation results (who may already be on the team in a different capacity). At the discretion of the parent or the agency, other individuals who have knowledge or special expertise regarding the child, including related services personnel. Additional language requires the representative of the LEA to be qualified to provide, or supervise the provision of specially designed instruction to meet the needs of children with disabilities, knowledgeable about the general education curriculum, and knowledgeable about the availability of LEA resources.

Development of the IEP. A new section in the law details what the IEP team must consider in developing each child's IEP. The IEP team must consider:

(i) the strengths of the child and the concerns of the parents for enhancing the education of their child;

(ii) the results of the initial evaluation or most recent evaluation.

(iii) As appropriate, the results of the child's performance on any general state or district-wide assessment programs.

Special factors to be considered include:

(a) in the case of a child whose behavior impedes his or her learning or that of others, the strategies, including positive behavioral interventions, strategies and supports needed to address that behavior;

(b) in the case of a child with limited English proficiency, the language needs of the child as they relate to the IEP;

(c) in the case of a child who is blind or visually impaired, provision of instruction in Braille and the use of Braille unless the IEP team determines that instruction in Braille or the use of Braille is not appropriate for the child;

(d) the communication needs of the child, and in the case of a child who is deaf or hard of hearing, consider the child's language and communication needs, opportunities for direct communications with peers and professional personnel in the child's language and communication mode, academic level, and full range of needs, including opportunities for direct instruction in the child's language and communication mode; and

(e) whether the child requires assistive technology devices and services.

General Education Teacher's Participation in IEP Development. Provisions require the general education teacher of the child, to the extent appropriate, to participate in the development of the IEP of the child and in the review and revision of the IEP, including the determination of appropriate positive behavioral interventions and strategies. Regulations clarify that the general education teacher must be part of the IEP team, but need not take part in every meeting or be present during throughout any meeting of the team.

Parents' Participation in Placement Decisions. A new provision in IDEA '97 requires that each LEA or SEA ensure that the parents of each child with a disability are members of any group that makes decisions on the educational placement of their child.

State Procedural Safeguards Requirements. P.L. 105-17 added procedures that SEAs, state agencies, or LEAs must establish and maintain. These include procedures related to mediation; procedures that require parents or the child's attorney to provide notice that a request for a due process has been made, including the name and residence of the child, a description of the nature of the problem of the child, and a proposed resolution of the problem; and procedures that require the SEA to develop a model form to assist parents in providing the notice mentioned above.

Parental Notice. In order to cut down on the repetitive information that is sent to parents, the Act divided information sent to parents into two notices: the prior written notice and the procedural safeguards notice.

Prior Written Notice. Agencies must provide prior written notice information to the parents of a child whenever there is a proposal to initiate or change (or refusal to initiate or change) the identification, evaluation, or educational placement of the child or the provision of a FAPE. The requirements of the information to be included in prior written notice includes:

    (a) a description of the action proposed or refused by the agency, and an explanation of why;

    (b) a description of other options that were considered and why those were rejected;

    (c) a description of each evaluation procedure, test record, or report the agency used as a basis for the proposed or refused action;

    (d) a description of other relevant factors;

    (e) a statement that the parents have protection under the procedural safeguards and, if the notice is not an initial referral for evaluation, the means by which a copy of a description of the procedural safeguards can be obtained; and

    (f) a list of sources for parents to contact to obtain assistance in understanding these provisions.

Procedural Safeguards Notice. A notice that includes information on procedural safeguards must be made available to the parents of a child with a disability upon initial referral for evaluation, upon each notification of an IEP meeting, upon reevaluation of the child, and upon registration of a complaint. This notice must include information relating to: independent educational evaluation, prior written notice, parental consent, access to educational records, opportunity to present complaints, the child's placement during pendency of due process proceedings, procedures for children who are subject to placement in an interim alternative educational setting, requirements for unilateral placement by parents of children in private schools at public expense, mediation, due process hearings, state-level appeals, civil action, and attorney's fees.

Mediation. A new section on mediation was included in the Act that requires SEAs and LEAs to ensure that procedures are established and implemented to allow parties to disputes to resolve disputes through a mediation process which, at a minimum, shall be available whenever a hearing is requested. The mediation process must be voluntary on the part of the parties, not used to deny or delay a parent's right to a due process hearing or to deny any other rights; and conducted by a qualified and impartial mediator trained in effective mediation techniques.

An LEA or SEA may establish procedures to require parents who choose not to use the mediation process to meet with a disinterested party who is under contract with a parent training and information center or community parent resource center or an appropriate alternative dispute resolution entity. The state must maintain a list of individuals who are qualified mediators and knowledgeable in laws and regulations relating to the provision of special education and related services. The state must also bear the cost of the mediation process. An agreement to the dispute in the mediation process must be set forth in a written mediation agreement. Provisions are also added to ensure that discussions that occur during the mediation must be confidential and not used as evidence in due process hearings or civil proceedings, and the parties may be required to sign a confidentiality pledge.

Requirement for Evaluation Information Prior to Due Process Hearings. The legislation requires that at least 5 business days prior to a hearing, each party must disclose to all other parties all evaluations completed by that date, and recommendations based on the offering party's evaluations that are intended to be used at the hearing.

Hearing Record and Written Findings of Fact and Decision. The Act clarifies the right to written, or at the option of the parents, an electronic verbatim record of the hearing, and findings of fact and decisions.

Attorneys' Fees. A provision is added that prohibits the award of attorneys' fees relating to any meeting of the IEP team unless the meeting is convened as a result of an administrative proceeding or judicial action, or, at the discretion of the state, for a mediation that is conducted prior to the filing of a complaint. An additional new provision allows attorneys' fees to be reduced if the attorney representing the parent did not provide required information to the school district.

Discipline of Children with Disabilities. IDEA '97 added substantive provisions that address the discipline of children with disabilities, including one allowing school personnel to order a change in the placement of a child with a disability to an appropriate interim alternative educational setting (IAES), another setting, or suspension, for not more than 10 school days (to the extent such alternative would be applied to children without disabilities).

Weapons and Drugs. A child that carries a weapon to school or to a school function, or who knowingly possesses or uses illegal drugs, or sells or solicits the sale of a controlled substance while at school or a school function can be placed in an IAES for the same amount of time that a child without a disability would be subject to discipline, but for not more than 45 days. The Department of Education, in non-binding guidance, suggests that a child who acquires a weapon while at school may also be covered under this provision.

Behavior Intervention Plan. The legislation requires that either before, or not later than 10 business days after either first removing the child for more than 10 school days in a school year or commencing a removal that constitutes a change of placement, the LEA must convene an IEP meeting to develop a functional behavioral assessment and implement a behavioral intervention plan to address the problem behavior (if the LEA did not conduct a functional behavioral assessment and implement a behavior intervention plan for the child before the problem behavior). If the child already has a behavior intervention plan, the IEP team shall review the plan and modify it, as necessary, to address the behavior.

Injury to Self or Others. A hearing officer may order a change in placement of a child with a disability to an IAES for not more than 45 days if the officer determines that the public agency has demonstrated by substantial evidence that maintaining the current placement of the child is substantially likely to result in injury to the child or to others, considers the appropriateness of the current placement, considers whether the agency has made reasonable efforts to minimize the risk of harm in the current placement (including the use of supplementary aids and services), and determines that the IAES meets the requirements set out below. The Department of Education, in non-binding guidance, suggests that changes of placement in such instances may also be available through a court order.

Interim Alternative Educational Setting (IAES). The Act requires the IAES to be determined by the IEP team and to be selected so as to enable the child to continue to participate in the general education curriculum although in another setting, continue to receive services and modifications, including those described in the child's current IEP, that will enable the child to meet the goals set out in that IEP. Provided services and modifications must also be designed to address the behavior that results in the child being removed from the child's current educational placement so that it does not recur.

Manifestation Determination Review. A manifestation determination is a review of the relationship between the child's disability and the behavior subject to the disciplinary action. If the result of the review is that the behavior was not a manifestation of the disability, the child may be disciplined in the same manner as a child without a disability, except exclusion (the cessation of all educational services) may not exceed 10 consecutive days or constitute a change in placement.

Manifestation determinations are required within 10 school days of any proposed change in placement for disciplinary reasons, including drugs, weapons, or a hearing officer's determination of risk of injury to self or others.

Requirements for Finding That Behavior s Not a Manifestation of the Disability. In carrying out this review, the IEP team may determine that the behavior of the child was not a manifestation of the child's disability only if the IEP team:
   (1) first considers, in terms of the behavior subject to disciplinary action, all relevant information, including
      (i) evaluation and diagnostic results, including the results or other relevant information supplied by the parents of the child;
      (ii) observations of the child; and
      (iii) the child's IEP and placement; and

(2) then determines that
    (j) in relationship to the behavior subject to disciplinary action, the child's IEP and placement were appropriate and the special education services, supplementary aids and services, and behavior intervention strategies were provided consistent with the child's IEP and placement;
    (ii) the child's disability did not impair the ability of the child to understand the impact and consequences of the behavior subject to disciplinary action; and
    (iii) the child's disability did not impair the ability of the child to control the behavior subject to disciplinary action.

Implications of Manifestation Review. If it is determined that the behavior of the child with a disability was not a manifestation of the child's disability, the relevant disciplinary procedures applicable to children without disabilities may be applied to the child in the same manner in which they would be applied to children without disabilities, except that children with disabilities must continue to receive a FAPE.

Parent Appeal and Child Placement During Appeal. New provisions allow parents who disagree with a determination that the child's behavior was not a manifestation of the disability, or with any decision regarding placement, to request a hearing. If they do, the SEA or LEA must arrange for an expedited hearing. During the appeal, the child shall remain in the IAES pending the decision of the hearing officer or until the expiration of the 45 day time limit, whichever occurs first, unless the parent and the SEA or LEA agree otherwise.

If a child is placed in an IAES and school personnel propose to change the child's placement after expiration of the IAES, the child shall remain in the current placement (the child's placement prior to the IAES) during the pendency of any proceeding to challenge the proposed change in placement, unless a hearing officer determines that there is substantial likelihood of injury to the child or to others for the child to return to the prior placement.

Children Not Yet Eligible for Special Education. A child who has not been determined to be eligible for special education and related services under IDEA and who has engaged in behavior that violated any rule or code of conduct of the LEA, may assert any of the protections provided in the IDEA if the LEA had knowledge that the child was a child with a disability before the behavior occurred. If the LEA did not have knowledge that the child was a child with a disability, the child may be subjected to the same disciplinary measures as applied to children without disabilities who engaged in comparable behaviors except as provided below. The LEA shall be deemed to have knowledge that the child is a child with a disability if:
    (a) the child's parent has expressed concern in writing (unless the parent is illiterate or has a disability that prevents compliance) to personnel of the appropriate educational agency that the child is in need of special education and related services;
    (b) the behavior or performance of the child demonstrates the need for such services;
    (c) the child's parent has requested an evaluation of the child under the IDEA; or
    (d) the teacher of the child, or other personnel of the LEA has expressed concern about the behavior or performance of the child to the director of special education or to other personnel of the agency in accordance with the agency's established child find procedures.

If a request is made for an evaluation of a child during the time in which the child is subjected to disciplinary measures, the evaluation shall be conducted in an expedited manner. If the child is determined to be a child with a disability, taking into consideration information from the evaluation conducted by the agency and information provided by the parents, the agency shall provide special education and related services in accordance with the provisions of Part B of IDEA, except that, pending the results of the evaluation the child shall remain in the educational placement determined by school authorities.

Referral to and Action by Law Enforcement. P.L. 105-17 clarifies that nothing prohibits an agency from reporting a crime committed by a child with a disability to appropriate authorities or prevents state law enforcement and judicial authorities from exercising their responsibilities with regard to the application of federal and state law to crimes committed by a child with a disability. An agency that reports a crime

Source: *IDEA 1997: Let's Make It Work,* 1999, Reston, VA: The Council For Exceptional Children

committed by a child with a disability must ensure that copies of the special education and disciplinary records of the child are transmitted for consideration by the appropriate authorities to whom it reports the crime.

Transfer of Parental Rights at Age of Majority. The legislation adds language that allows a state to require that, when a child with a disability reaches the age of majority under state law (except for a child with a disability who has been determined to be incompetent under state law):

(a) the public agency provide a notice to both the individual and parents,
(b) transfer all rights accorded to parents to the child, and
(c) notify the individual and parents of the transfer of rights. All rights must be transferred to children who are incarcerated in an adult or juvenile federal, state, or local correctional institution.

For children who have reached the age of majority who have not been determined to be incompetent, but who are determined not to have the ability to provide informed consent with respect to the educational program of the child, the state will establish procedures for the appointment of the parent of the child, or if the parent is not available, of another appropriate individual to represent the educational interest of the child throughout the period of eligibility of the child under IDEA.

Withholding Funds from States. The Act allows the Federal government to withhold part or all of a state's payment if there is a failure to substantially comply with requirements.

Program Information. New provisions require states to provide information on the number of children with disabilities by race and ethnicity, who from birth through age 2, stopped receiving early intervention services because of program completion or for other reasons; the number of children, by race, ethnicity, and disability category, who are removed to an IAES and the acts or items precipitating those removals; the number of children with disabilities subject to long-term suspensions or expulsions; and the number of infants and toddlers, by race and ethnicity, at risk of having substantial developmental delays who are receiving early intervention services.

Race Disproportionality. New provisions require that each state collect and examine data to determine if significant disproportionality based on race is occurring in a state in relation to the identification of children as children with disabilities. They must also determine if children of different racial groups are disproportionately represented in each of the disability categories or in each type of educational setting. In the case of a determination of significant disproportionality, the state must provide for the review and, if appropriate, revision of policies and practices used in identification or placement to ensure compliance with the Act.

Preschool Program. The new legislation replaces language authorizing a maximum of $1,500 for each eligible child with a flat authorization of $500 million for fiscal year 1998 and such sums as necessary for each subsequent fiscal year. As noted before, the preschool formula also changed. For state administration and state-level activities, the legislation is changed to allow states to retain an amount equal to 25% of the amount the state received for fiscal year 1997 plus future increases at the lesser of the rate of inflation or Federal appropriations increases.

State Preschool Activities. State preschool activities may include among other things: support services which may benefit children with disabilities younger than age 3 or older than age 5 as long as those services also benefit children with disabilities aged 3 through 5; direct services; development of a state improvement plan; activities to meet the performance goals and to support implementation of the state improvement plan; supplements to other funds used to develop and implement a state-wide coordinated services system (not to exceed 1% of the amount received by the state under this section for a fiscal year).

III. Part C: Infants and Toddlers with Disabilities

Infants and Toddlers at Risk for Developmental Delay. The policy section of the infants and toddlers program was expanded to encourage states to expand opportunities for children under 3 years of age who would be at risk of having substantial developmental delays if they did not receive early intervention services. Additional changes in the state application provisions require a state to provide a description of the uses of services to at-risk infants and toddlers if the state provides such services.

The requirements governing the use of funds were modified to allow any state that did not provide services for at-risk infants and toddlers to strengthen the state-wide system by initiating, expanding, or improving collaborative efforts related to at-risk infants and toddlers, including establishing linkages with appropriate community-based organizations, services, and personnel for identifying and evaluating at-risk infants and toddlers, making referrals, and conducting periodic follow-up on each referral.

State Eligibility. The state eligibility section was changed to permit states to be eligible for a grant if they have adopted a policy that demonstrates that appropriate early intervention services are available to all infants and toddlers with disabilities in the state and their families, including Indian infants and toddlers with disabilities and their families residing on a reservation geographically located in the state, and have in effect a state-wide system that meets the requirements for Part C.

Requirements of a State-Wide System. Changes are made that allow states to include the training of personnel to work in rural and inner-city areas (CSPD), and to establish policies and procedures to ensure that to the maximum extent appropriate, early intervention services are provided in natural environments and that services that are provided in a setting other than a natural environment occur only when early intervention cannot be achieved satisfactorily in a natural environment.

Personnel Recruitment and Hiring. The Act allows a state to adopt a policy that includes making ongoing good-faith efforts to recruit and hire appropriately and adequately trained personnel to provide services to infants and toddlers with disabilities, including, in a geographic area of the state where there is a shortage of personnel, the most qualified individuals available who are making progress toward completing applicable course work necessary within 3 years, to meet the state's standards.

Individualized Family Service Plan (IFSP). A change in the requirements on the content of the IFSP requires a justification of the extent, if any, to which early intervention services will not be provided in a natural environment.

Transition from Early Intervention Services to Preschool and Other Appropriate Services. The legislation makes changes in the state application provisions to allow a conference to be convened among the lead agency, the family, and the LEA at least 90 days (and at the discretion of all parties up to 6 months) before the child is eligible for preschool services; and in the case of a child who may not be eligible for preschool services, allows the lead agency to make reasonable efforts to convene a conference to discuss the appropriate services that the child may receive at age 3.

Previous State Application. A new provision allows states to be eligible if they already have a state application on file that remains in effect. The Secretary may require a state to modify its application if there is an amendment to the Act, a new interpretation, or an official finding of noncompliance.

Mediation. The procedural safeguards required to be included in a state-wide system are expanded to include the right of parents to use mediation.

State Interagency Coordinating Council (SICC). The legislation makes changes to the requirements governing the SICC. There is no longer a minimum and maximum number of members required or a specific requirement to include minority parents. A representative from a Head Start agency or program in the state and a representative from a state agency responsible for child care now must also be on the council. The SICC is also authorized to advise appropriate agencies in the state with respect to the integration of services for infants and toddlers and at-risk infants and toddlers and their families, regardless of whether at-risk infants and toddlers are eligible for early intervention services in the state.

State Formula. A special rule is added for 1998 and 1999 that requires no state to receive an amount that is less than the sum of the amounts the state received for fiscal year 1994 under Part H as then in effect and Subpart 2 of Part D of Chapter 1 of Title I of the Elementary and Secondary Education Act of 1965 (state-operated or supported programs for children with disabilities and for children with disabilities under 3 years of age. An exception is made if the number of infants and toddlers in the state is less than the number of infants and toddlers reported by the state for fiscal year 1994, in which case the amount will be reduced by the same percentage by which the number of infants and toddlers declined.

If the funds appropriated are insufficient to pay the full amount that all states are eligible to receive, the Secretary will ratably reduce the allocations. If there are additional funds, the Secretary will increase funds on the same basis they were reduced.

Federal Interagency Coordinating Council (FICC). The membership of the FICC is expanded to include a representative of the Office of Educational Research and Improvement and a representative of the Head Start Bureau of the Administration for Children and Families. A provision requiring three parents is changed to eliminate the number specification but requires that parents constitute 20% of the Council. The activities of the Council are expanded to allow the Council to advise and assist not only the Secretary of Education but also the Secretaries of Health and Human Services, Defense, Interior, and Agriculture, and the Commissioner of Social Security.

Authorization of Appropriations. The program is now authorized $400 million for fiscal year 1998 and such sums as necessary for each of the fiscal years 1999 through 2002.

IV. Part D: National Activities to Improve Education of Children with Disabilities Consolidation of Discretionary Programs Into the New Part D.

The legislation consolidates and changes authorities previously under the Parts C through G into a New Part D. There are no authorization levels included under Part D. All programs are to be authorized "at such sums as necessary." Part D has two subparts: Subpart 1: State Program Improvement Grants for Children with Disabilities and Subpart 2: Coordinated Research, Personnel Preparation, Technical Assistance, Support, and Dissemination of Information. Subpart 2 includes two chapters: Chapter 1: Improving Early Intervention, Educational, and Transitional Services and Results for Children with Disabilities Through Coordinated Research and Personnel Preparation; and Chapter 2: Improving Early Intervention, Educational, and Transitional Services and Results for Children with Disabilities Through Coordinated Technical Assistance, Support, and Dissemination of Information.

Subpart 1: State Program Improvement Grants for Children with Disabilities

State Program Improvement Grants. A new competitive grant program authorizes the Secretary to make grants of not less than $500,000 or more than $2 million to SEAs for not less than a year and not more than 5 years to reform and improve their systems for providing educational, early intervention, and transitional services, including their systems for professional development, technical assistance, and dissemination of knowledge about best practices.

State Partnership for Improvement Grants. In order to be eligible, an SEA must establish a partnership with LEAs and other state agencies involved in or concerned with the education of children with disabilities. Partners must include the governor, parents of children with and without disabilities, individuals with disabilities, organizations representing individuals with disabilities and their parents (such as parent training and information centers), community-based and other nonprofit organizations involved in the education and employment of individuals with disabilities, the lead state agency for Part C, general and special education teachers, the state advisory panel, the SICC, and institutions of higher education within the state. A partnership may also include individuals knowledgeable about vocational education, the state agency for higher education, the state vocational rehabilitation agency, public agencies with jurisdiction in the areas of health, mental health, social service, and juvenile justice, and other individuals.

Requirements for Analyses of State Information. To receive a grant, the SEA's application must include a plan that includes an analysis of:

- All information reasonably available on the performance of children with disabilities;
- State and local needs for professional development for personnel to serve children with disabilities;
- Major findings of the most recent reviews of state compliance as they related to improving results; and
- Other information on the effectiveness of the state's systems of early intervention, special education, and general education in meeting the needs of children with disabilities.

Use of State Improvement Funds. An SEA must also describe how funds will be used for systemic-change activities and the strategies the state will use to address identified needs, including how the state will change policies and procedures to address systemic barriers; hold LEAs and schools accountable for educational progress of children with disabilities; provide technical assistance to LEAs and schools; and address the identified needs for inservice and preservice preparation of professionals and paraprofessionals, including how the state will:

- Prepare general and special education personnel with needed content knowledge and the collaborative skills (including how the state will work with other states on common certification criteria);
- Prepare professional and paraprofessionals in early intervention personnel in needed content knowledge and collaborative skills;
- Work with institutions of higher education and other entities to ensure they develop the capacity to support quality professional development programs that meet state and local needs;
- Work to develop collaborative agreements with other states for joint support and development of programs to prepare personnel;
- Work in collaboration with other states to address the lack of uniformity and reciprocity in the credentialing of teachers and other personnel;
- Enhance the ability of teachers and others to use strategies to address the conduct of children with disabilities that impedes learning;
- Acquire and disseminate educational research findings to school personnel and adopt promising practices, materials, and technology;
- Recruit, prepare, and retain qualified personnel that are underrepresented in the fields of general and special education, and related services;
- Ensure that the plan is integrated with other professional development plans and activities; and
- Provide for joint training of parents, general and special education teachers, and related services personnel.

An SEA must also describe strategies that will address identified systemic programs needs (including shortages of qualified personnel), how the state will disseminate results of the local capacity-building and improvement projects, how the state will address improving results for children with disabilities in the geographic areas of greatest need; and how the state will regularly assess which strategies have been effective.

Professional Development Fund Requirement. An SEA that receives State Program Improvement Grants is required to use not less than 75% of funds to ensure that there are enough general education, special education, and related service personnel who have the skills and knowledge necessary to meet the needs of children with disabilities, or to work with other states on common certification criteria. If a state can demonstrate that it has the personnel needed, the state may use not less than 50% of the funds for these purposes.

Subpart 2: Coordinated Research, Personnel Preparation, Technical Assistance, Support, and Dissemination of Information

Comprehensive Plan. Under Subpart 2, the Secretary is authorized to develop and implement a plan for activities designed to enhance the educational and related services of children with disabilities. The Secretary must consult with individuals with disabilities, parents of children with disabilities, appropriate professions, and representatives of SEAs, LEAs, institutions of higher education, private schools, and others in developing the plan.

Grants for Activities. A new program authorizes grants for SEAs, LEAs, institutions of higher education, any other public agency, private nonprofits, outlying areas, Indian tribes, or for-profit organizations, for activities to enhance the provision of education, related services, transition, and early intervention services to children with disabilities under Parts B and C. Projects must involve individuals with disabilities or parents of individuals with disabilities in planning, implementing, and evaluating the project. The Secretary must ensure funds are for activities that are designed to benefit children with disabilities, their families, or the personnel employed to work with them or to benefit other individuals with disabilities. Priorities will be given to projects that:

- Address one or more of the following: age ranges, disabilities, school grades, types of educational placements or early intervention environments, types of services, content areas (such as reading), or effective strategies for helping children with disabilities learn appropriate behavior;
- Projects that address the needs of children based on the severity of their disability;
- Projects that address the needs of: low-achieving children, underserved populations, children from low-income families, children with limited English proficiency, unserved and underserved areas, particular types of geographic areas, or children whose behavior interferes with their learning and socialization;
- Projects to reduce inappropriate identification of children, particularly among minority children;
- Projects that are carried out in particular areas of the country, to ensure broad geographic coverage; and
- Any activity that is expressly authorized in Chapters 1 or 2.

Additional Requirements for Projects. The Secretary may require a recipient of the grant to share in the cost of the project, to prepare research and evaluation findings and products in formats for specific audiences, to disseminate the findings and products, and to collaborate with other recipients.

Panel to Evaluate Applications for Projects. A standing panel is established to evaluate applications for projects. The panel will include representatives of institutions of higher education that have programs of personnel preparation, individuals who design and carry out programs of research targeted at the improvement of special education, individuals who have recognized experience and knowledge necessary to integrate and apply research findings to improve results for children with disabilities, individuals who administer programs for children with disabilities, individuals who prepare parents of children with disabilities to participate in making decisions about the education of their children, individuals who establish policies that affect the delivery of services to children with disabilities, parents of children with disabilities, and individuals with disabilities. Individuals can serve on the panel for no more than 3 consecutive years, unless the Secretary deems it necessary. The Secretary may use not more than 1% of the funds under this subpart to pay for non-Federal administrative support related to the management of applications.

Reservation of Funds for the Secretary. The Secretary is authorized to use up to 20% of funds available under either Chapters 1 or 2 to carry out activities or combinations of activities across all of the authorities of Chapters 1 and 2, namely: research; personnel preparation; parent training and information; technical assistance and dissemination; technology development, demonstration, and utilization; or media services.

Funds to Address Children from Minority Backgrounds and for HBCUs. The Secretary will, as appropriate, require an application for a grant to demonstrate how the needs of children with disabilities from minority backgrounds will be addressed. The Secretary will also ensure that at least 1% of funds will be used for outreach and technical assistance to Historically Black Colleges and Universities (HBCUs) and to institutions of higher education with minority enrollments of at least 25%.

Special Funding Requirements. The legislation specifies a certain level of funds be appropriated to address the following needs: $12,832,000 to address the needs of children with deaf-blindness; $4 million to address the post-secondary, vocational, technical, continuing and adult education needs of individuals with deafness; and $4 million to address the needs of children with an emotional disturbance, and those who are at risk of developing an emotional disturbance. A provision indicates that if the total amount appropriated to carry out activities related to research, personnel preparation, and coordinate technical assistance and dissemination sections is less than $130 million, the amounts will be ratably reduced.

Chapter 1: Improving Early Intervention, Educational, and Transitional Services and Results for Children with Disabilities Through Coordinated Research and Personnel Preparation

Research and Innovation. The Secretary is required to make competitive grants to improve the practices of professionals and others providing services to children with disabilities and to improve the educational results for children with disabilities; to address the special needs of preschool-aged children and infant and toddlers with disabilities, including those at-risk of having substantial developmental delays; to address the specific programs of overidentification and underidentification of children with disabilities; to develop and implement effective strategies for addressing inappropriate behavior of children with disabilities in schools; to improve secondary and post-secondary education and transitional services for children with disabilities; and to address the range of needs of children with disabilities who need significant levels of support to maximize their participation and learning in school and in the community. Specific authorized activities are listed under New Knowledge Production, Integration of Research and Practice, and Improving the Use of Professional Knowledge.

- **New Knowledge Production.** The Secretary is required to support activities that lead to the production of new knowledge through activities that will: expand understanding of the relationships between learning characteristics of children with disabilities and their diverse backgrounds; develop or identify innovative effective, and efficient curricula designs, instructional approaches, and strategies; advance the design of assessment tools and procedures that will accurately and efficiently determine the special needs of children with disabilities, especially within the context of general education; study and promote improved alignment and compatibility of general and special education reform; advance the design, development, and integration of technology, assistive technology devices, media, and materials; improve designs, processes, and results of personnel preparation for personnel who provide services to children with disabilities through the acquisition of information on, and implementation of, research-based practices; and advance knowledge about the coordination of education with health and social services.

- **Integration of Research and Practice.** The Secretary is required to support activities that integrate research and practice, including activities that support state systemic-change and local capacity-building and improvement efforts, including:
  (a) model demonstration projects to apply and test research findings to determine the usability and effectiveness of research findings;
  (b) activities to demonstrate and apply research-based findings to facilitate systemic changes;
  (c) activities to promote and demonstrate the coordination of early intervention and educational services for children with disabilities with services provided by health, rehabilitation, and social service agencies; and (d) activities to identify and disseminate solutions that overcome systemic barriers to effective and efficient service delivery.

- **Improving the Use of Professional Knowledge.** The Secretary is required to support activities that improve the use of professional knowledge, including activities that synthesize useful research and other information relating to the provision of service to children with disabilities; analyze professional knowledge bases to advance an understanding of the relationships, and the effectiveness of practice relating to the provision of services; ensure that research and related products are in appropriate formats for distribution; enable professionals, parents of children with disabilities, and other persons, to learn about and implement the findings of research and successful practices developed in model demonstration projects; and conduct outreach, and dissemination information relating to successful approaches to overcoming systemic barriers to the effective and efficient delivery of services, to personnel who provide services.

Balance Among Activities and Age Ranges in Research and Innovation Grants. The Secretary must ensure that there is an appropriate balance among knowledge production, integration of research and practice, and use of professional knowledge and across all age ranges of children with disabilities.

Source: *IDEA 1997: Let's Make It Work,* 1999, Reston, VA: The Council For Exceptional Children

Personnel Preparation. This section requires the Secretary to make competitive grants to help address state-identified needs for qualified personnel in special education, related services, early intervention, and general education, to work with children with disabilities and to ensure that the personnel have needed skills and knowledge. Specific authorized activities are listed for

(a) preparing personnel to work with low-incidence disabilities;
(b) leadership preparation;
(c) projects of national significance; and
(d) preparing personnel to work with children with high-incidence disabilities.

- **Low-Incidence Disabilities**. The Secretary is required to support activities that benefit children with low-incidence disabilities, including:
  (a) preparing persons who have prior training in educational and other related service fields and are studying to obtain degrees, certificates, or licensure that will enable them to assist children and infants and toddlers with disabilities in meeting their objectives;
  (b) providing personnel from various disciplines with interdisciplinary training;
  (c) preparing personnel in the innovative uses and application of technology;
  (d) preparing personnel who provide services to children with visual impairments to teach and use Braille;
  (e) preparing personnel to be qualified educational interpreters; and
  (f) preparing personnel who provide services to children with significant cognitive disabilities and children with multiple disabilities.

- **Leadership Preparation**. The Secretary is required to support leadership preparation activities, including preparing personnel at the advanced graduate, doctoral, and postdoctoral levels of training to administer, enhance or provide services for children with disabilities; and providing interdisciplinary training for various types of leadership personnel.

- **Projects of National Significance**. The Secretary is required to support activities that are of a national significance and have broad applicability, including:
  (a) developing and demonstrating effective and efficient practices for preparing personnel to provide services, including practices that address any needs identified in the state's improvement plan;
  (b) demonstrating the application of significant knowledge derived from research and other sources in the development of programs to prepare personnel;
  (c) demonstrating models for the preparation of, and interdisciplinary training of, special education and general education personnel to enable them to acquire needed collaboration skills and to achieve results that meet challenging standards (particularly within the general education curriculum);
  (d) demonstrating models that reduce shortages of teachers and personnel from other relevant disciplines, through reciprocity arrangements between states that are related to licensure and certification;
  (e) developing, evaluating, and disseminating model teaching standards for persons working with children with disabilities;
  (f) promoting the transferability of licensure and certification;
  (g) developing and disseminating models that prepare teachers with strategies for addressing the conduct of children with disabilities that impede learning;
  (h) institutes that provide professional development that addresses the needs of children with disabilities to teachers or teams of teachers, and where appropriate, to school boards and other school personnel;
  (i) projects to improve the ability of general education teachers, principals and other administrators to meet the needs of children with disabilities;
  (j) developing, evaluating, and disseminating innovative models for the recruitment, induction, retention, and assessment of new, qualified teachers, especially those from underrepresented groups; and
  (k) supporting institutions of higher education with minority enrollment of at least 25% for the purpose of preparing personnel to work with children with disabilities.

- **High Incidence Disabilities**. The Secretary is required to support activities to benefit children with high-incidence disabilities, including:
  (a) activities undertaken by institutions of higher education, LEAs, and other local entities to improve and reform their existing program to prepare teachers and related services personnel to meet the diverse needs of children with disabilities and to work collaboratively in general education

classroom settings and to incorporate best practices and research-based knowledge about preparing personnel;

(b) activities incorporating innovative strategies to recruit and prepare teachers and other personnel to meet the needs of areas in which there are shortages of personnel; and

(c) activities designed to develop career opportunities for paraprofessionals to receive training as special education teachers, related services personnel, and early intervention personnel.

Requirement for State Involvement in Personnel Preparation Grants. The legislation requires that any application for personnel preparation grants include information demonstrating that the activities described will address needs identified by the state and if the applicant is not an SEA or LEA, information demonstrating that one or more SEAs have engaged in a cooperative effort to plan the project and will cooperate in carrying out and monitoring the project. The Secretary may also require applicants to provide letters from one or more states declaring that the states intend to accept successful completion of the programs as meeting state personnel standards and need personnel in the area or areas in which the applicant proposed to provide preparation.

Personnel Preparation Requirements That Applicants Must Meet State and Professional Standards. The Secretary will only make grants to eligible applicants that meet state and professionally recognized standards for the preparation of special education and related services personnel, if the purpose of the project is to assist personnel in obtaining degrees.

Preferences for Personnel Preparation Grants. The Secretary may give preference to institutions of higher education that are educating general education personnel to meet the needs of children with disabilities in integrated settings and educating special education personnel to work in collaboration with general educators in integrated settings; and give preference to institutions that are successfully recruiting and preparing individuals with disabilities and individuals from groups that are underrepresented.

Personnel Preparation Service Obligation. Each application for a personnel preparation grant must include an assurance that the applicant will ensure that individuals who receive a scholarship will provide special education and related services to children with disabilities for a period of 2 years for every year the assistance was received or repay all or part of the cost of the assistance. For applicants who receive funds for leadership preparation, the applicant must ensure that individuals who receive a scholarship will perform work related to their preparation for a period of 2 years for every year assistance was received or repay all or part of the costs.

Studies and Evaluations. The legislation requires grants to assess the effectiveness of state and local efforts to provide a FAPE to children with disabilities and early intervention services to both infants and toddlers with disabilities and infants and toddlers at risk of having substantial developmental delays. The Secretary is authorized to support studies, evaluations, and assessments, including studies that analyze measurable impact, outcomes, and results achieved by the SEAs and LEAs; analyze state and local needs for professional development, parent training, and other appropriate activities that can reduce the need for disciplinary actions involving children with disabilities; assess services and results for children with disabilities from minority backgrounds; measure services and results for children with disabilities, including longitudinal studies; and identify and report on the placement of children with disabilities by disability category.

- **National Assessment.** The Secretary is required to carry out a national assessment of activities in consultations with researchers, practitioners, parents of children with disabilities, individuals with disabilities and others. The national assessment will examine how well schools, LEAs, SEAs, and other recipients of assistance are achieving the purposes of the legislation.
- **Annual Report.** The Secretary must report annually to the Congress on the findings and determinations resulting from reviews of state implementation.
- **Technical Assistance to LEAs.** The Secretary is required to make grants to LEAs to assist them in carrying out local capacity-building and improvement projects.
- **Authorization of Funds for Studies and Technical Assistance.** The Secretary may reserve up to one half of 1% of the amount appropriate under parts B and C for this part. Half of the funds must be used for technical assistance.

Chapter 2: Improving Early Intervention, Educational, and Transitional Services and Results for Children with Disabilities Through Coordinated Technical Assistance, Support, and Dissemination of Information.

Parent Training and Information Centers (PTICs). There are some changes to the provisions governing grants to parent training and information centers in the new legislation. The Secretary must make at least one award to a parent organization in each state, unless no application from an organization of sufficient quality is received. Required activities now include:

    (a) helping parents to understand the availability of, and how to effectively use procedural safeguards, including encouraging the use, and explaining the benefits of alternative methods of dispute resolution, such as the mediation process;

    (b) assisting parents in participating in school reform activities;

    (c) contracting with SEAs to provide individuals who meet with parents to explain the mediation process to them; and

    (d) networking with appropriate clearinghouses. Annual reporting requirements are reduced to require the reporting of the number of parents to whom it provided information and training and the effectiveness of strategies that were used to reach and serve parents, including underserved parents.

- **Optional Activities.** PTICs may also provide information to teachers and other professionals, assist children with disabilities in understanding their rights on reaching the age of majority, and assist parents in becoming informed participants in the development and implementation of the state improvement plan.

Community Parent Resource Centers. A new section authorizes grants to local parent organizations to support PTICs that will help ensure that underserved parents of children with disabilities have the training and information they need.

Technical Assistance for PTICs. The new legislation identifies authorized activities that are allowable in the technical assistance the Secretary provides to PTICs.

Coordinated Technical Assistance and Dissemination. The Secretary is required to make grants to provide technical assistance and information through such mechanisms as institutes, regional resource centers, clearinghouses, and programs that support states and local entities in building capacity to improve services and results for children with disabilities and their families.

- **Systemic Technical Assistance.** The Secretary is required to support technical assistance activities relating to systemic change, including:

    (a) assisting SEAs, LEAs, and other participants in partnerships with the process of planning systemic changes;

    (b) promoting change through a multistate or regional framework;

    (c) increasing the depth and utility of information in ongoing and emerging areas of priority needs identified by SEAs, LEAs, and other participants in partnerships; and

    (d) promoting communication and information exchange among SEAs, LEAs, and other participants in partnerships.

- **Specialized Technical Assistance.** The Secretary is required to support activities relating to areas of priority or specific populations, including activities that:

    (a) focus on specific areas of high-priority need;

    (b) focus on needs and issues that are specific to a population of children with disabilities, such as schools and agencies serving children with deaf-blindness and to programs and agencies serving other groups of children with low-incidence disabilities and their families; or

    (c) address the post-secondary education needs of individuals who are deaf or hard of hearing.

- **National Information Dissemination.** The Secretary is required to support information and dissemination activities, including activities relating to:

    (a) infants and toddlers with disabilities and their families, and children with disabilities and their families;

(b) services for populations of children with low-incidence disabilities, including children with deaf-blindness and targeted age groupings;

(c) the provision of post-secondary services;

(d) the need for and use of personnel to provide services, and personnel recruitment, retention, and preparation;

(e) issues that are of critical interest to SEAs and LEAs, other agency personnel, parents of children with disabilities, and individuals with disabilities;

(f) educational reform and systemic change within states; and

(g) promoting schools that are safe and conducive to learning.

- **Linking States to Information Sources.** The Secretary may also support projects that link states to technical assistance resources and may make research and related products available through libraries, electronic networks, parent training projects, and other information sources.

Authorization of Appropriations for Part D Activities. The legislation does not authorize a specific level of funds for the Part D activities but instead authorizes such sums as may be necessary for each of the fiscal years 1998 through 2002.

Technology Development, Demonstration, and Utilization, and Educational Media Services. The legislation retains grant authority for technology development and educational media activities in this section. There is no specific level of funds authorized but such sums as necessary are authorized for each of the fiscal years 1998 through 2002.

- **Technology Activities.** The Secretary is required to make competitive grants to support activities to promote the development, demonstration, and utilization of technology, including activities such as:

(a) conducting research and development activities on the use of innovative and emerging technologies;

(b) promoting the demonstration and use of innovative and emerging technologies by improving and expanding the transfer of technology from research and development to practice;

(c) providing technical assistance to recipients of other assistance, concerning the development of accessible, effective, and usable products;

(d) communicating information on available technology and uses of technology to assist children with disabilities;

(e) supporting the implementation of research programs on captioning or video description;

(f) supporting research, development, and dissemination to technology with universal-design features; and

(g) demonstrating the use of publicly-funded telecommunication systems to provide parents and teachers with information and training concerning early diagnosis of, intervention for, and effective teaching strategies for young children with reading disabilities.

- **Educational Media Services.** The required activities include:

(a) educational media activities that are designed to be of educational value to children with disabilities;

(b) providing video description, open captioning, or closed captioning of television programs, videos, or educational materials through September 30, 2001, and after fiscal year 2001, providing video description, open captioning, or closed captioning of educational, news, and informational television, videos, or materials;

(c) distributing captioned and described videos or educational materials through such mechanisms as a loan service;

(d) providing free educational materials in accessible media for children with visual impairments in elementary, secondary, post-secondary, and graduate schools;

(e) providing cultural experiences through appropriate nonprofit organizations, such as the National Theater of the Deaf, that enrich the lives of children and adults with hearing impairments and increase public awareness and understanding of deafness; and

(f) compiling and analyzing appropriate data related to the activities.

Effective Dates. Parts A and B, except for the following, shall take effect upon the enactment of the Act (upon President's signature): Sec. 617 (Administration) shall take effect on October 1, 1997; Sec. 612(a)(4) (IEP) shall take effect on July 1, 1998; Sec. 612(a)(14) (CSPD) shall take effect on July 1, 1998; Sec. 612(a)(16) (Performance Goals and Indicators) shall take effect on July 1, 1998; Sec. 614(d) IEP shall take effect on July 1, 1998, except for paragraph (6), provisions for children with disabilities in adult prisons, which takes effect upon enactment; Sec. 618 (Program Information/Data Collection) shall take effect on July 1, 1998; Sec. 611 and 619 shall take effect beginning with funds appropriated for FY 98.

- **Part D-Support Programs**: Changes to the support programs go into effect on October 1, 1997, except for the following. Paragraphs 1 and 2 of Sec. 661(g) (Standing Panel and Peer Review Panels) shall take effect on January 1, 1998. Beginning October 1, 1997, the Secretary of Education may use funds appropriated under Part D to make continuation awards for projects that were funded under Sec. 618 and Parts C through G of IDEA as in effect on September 30, 1997.
- **Part C** (formerly Part H-Early Intervention) shall take effect on July 1, 1998.
- **Part I** (Family Support Program) is repealed as of October 1, 1998.

Authorization to Continue to Fund Continuation Grants. A provision is included that allows the Secretary to use funds appropriated under Part D to make continuation awards for projects that were funded previously under Parts C through G as in effect on September 30, 1997.

Videos from CEC's Satellite Broadcasts

Implementing IDEA '97
IEPs That Work for Everyone

This video demonstrates the practical details of what to include in the IEP and how to address assessment of present levels of performance, developing measurable goals, strategies for collaborative goal setting with family members, general education teachers, and other members of the team. Presenters are Mary Watson of the North Carolina Department of Public Instruction and Nancy Johnson of the University of North Carolina. The video package includes reproducible materials for participant activities.
#M5317 VHS 1999 Approximately 2 hours Closed captioned $149 CEC Members $109

Implementing IDEA '97
Get Disciplined! Addressing Student Challenging Behavior

This video provides information on how to use a multi-level approach to discipline that helps teachers set limits and manage student behavior in school-wide settings. Examples and participant activities include ways to identify and eliminate trouble spots in your school. The discussion focuses on targeted interventions, functional assessments, intervention plans, and intensive interventions. The presenters are C. Michael Nelson and Terrence Scott of the University of Kentucky Department of Special Education and Rehabilitation. The tape also includes a brief overview of the Federal Regulations presented by CEC's Assistant Executive Director for Public Policy, Joseph Ballard. The video package includes reproducible materials for participant activities.
#M5318 VHS 1999 Approximately 2.5 hours Closed captioned $149 CEC Members $109

IDEA Reauthorization:
Major Features of the New Law

This general overview provides an invaluable resource for examining the basic changes of the law including procedural safeguards/parent involvement, evaluation/reevaluation, early childhood and developmental delay, curriculum, and discipline management. Presenters: Linda M. Lewis, Joseph Ballard, Lynn Malarz, Michael Opuda, and Jo Thomason
#M5246 VHS 1997 Approximately 3 hours Closed Captioned $149 CEC Members $109

IDEA Reauthorization:
Focus on the IEP and Performance Assessment

Hear what experts have to say about student involvement, performance assessment, benchmarks/short term objectives, accommodations, alternative assessment, and involving the general education teacher.
Presenters: Joseph Ballard, Pat Guthrie, Jonathan C. McIntire, Margaret McLaughlin, Alba Ortiz, and Martha Thurlow.
#M5248 VHS 1998 Approximately 3 hours Closed Captioned $149 CEC Members $109

IDEA Reauthorization:
Discipline and Creating Positive Learning Environments

This video answers questions about IDEA requirements concerning the role of the IEP team, behavioral intervention plans, suspension and expulsion, and Interim Alternative Education Settings. Also discussed are positive behavioral supports, cultural differences in relation to behavior, and developing safe schools.
#M5278 VHS 1998 Approximately 3 hours Closed Captioned $149 CEC Members $109

IDEA 1997 Resources

Preliminary Analysis: The Law and Regulations
IDEA 1997: Let's Make It Work
CEC Public Policy Unit

This update of the 1998 version of the book includes the fine points of the law as determined by the regulations, which were issued on March 12, 1999. This document informs the reader about both statutory and regulatory elements for 15 topical areas through an easy-to-read question and answer format. It also includes an updated summary of IDEA. The content of this publication was developed by a team of policy experts, who were able to come together at CEC headquarters within hours of the issuance of the regulations.
#R5235P 1999 97pp $14.95 CEC Members $10.50

IEP Team Guide
The Council for Exceptional Children

This book provides a step-by-step analysis of what the law requires in developing the IEP and how the IEP team can work together to ensure a well rounded and responsive program for children with disabilities. In clear, concise, everyday language it explains what federal law requires and guides the user through the process of developing and revising an IEP. Most importantly, it explains the value and role of each team member and provides checklists of how each person can best be prepared to participate at the IEP team meeting.
#P5274 1999 115pp $29.95 CEC Members $20.95

Prices may change without notice.
To order call toll-free 1-888-232-7733
24-hour Fax 703-264-9494